Not So Prim Rose

The complete misadventures
of **Rose Bush,** *Flower* magazine's
irreverent editor

WRITTEN BY **MARGOT SHAW** • FOREWORD BY **JULIA REED** • ILLUSTRATIONS BY **CLAIRE CORMANY**

Printed in the U.S.A.
ISBN 978-0-9846864-0-7

Author: MARGOT SHAW
Illustrator: CLAIRE CORMANY
Cover Designer: ELLEN S. PADGETT
Page Designer: JENA HIPPENSTEEL
Copy Editor: ABBY BRASWELL

First Printing: 2011

Published by
Peony Publishing LLC
Birmingham, AL 35243
205-970-9775
Flowermag.com

All essays first appeared in

FLOWER

HOUSE | GARDEN | LIFESTYLE

To read Rose Bush is to learn the key to a profoundly happy life: Always be brave enough to laugh—first and hardest—at yourself.

SHE'S SHARP AND SELF-DEPRECATING, FILLED WITH compassion, and outfitted with a keen eye for the telling detail. In short she's possessed of my very favorite brand of humor, and she can tell a story like nobody's business.

Devoted readers of her delightful column will recognize the characters who populate her extraordinarily full daily life: assorted intrepid *Flower* girls, an often maniacal menagerie of dogs and cats, the dreamy MacGyver of a husband who also happens to be a minister (Who could ask for a better combo that that?). With their help, Rose manages to navigate life and all its manifold travails—including lost keys and botched schedules, ill-timed cold snaps and epic rainstorms, hipster hotels, and technological challenges—with grit and aplomb and a smile (almost always) on her face.

In the end, she convinces her readers that there's very little that a stout heart, an irrepressible glass-half-full outlook, a quick prayer, and a Motown soundtrack can't defeat. The perfect cure for the everyday blues, this collection is a must-read for anyone who needs a good laugh or a healthy shot of optimism. And isn't that all of us?

–JULIA REED, AUTHOR

Table of Contents

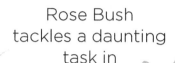

Rose Bush
tackles a daunting
task in

nightmare at the museum

AS MANY OF YOU KNOW, Birmingham is a veritable hotbed of flowering folks—male and female. Historically, I have not been among them. But about four years ago I fell head over heels in love with flowering and have not wavered in my affections since.

Imagine my shock and awe when I got the call to participate in "Art in Bloom"—the biannual Birmingham Museum of Art event where flower artists interpret works of art in the museum collection and/or, in the case of 2006, several Comme des Garçons dresses.

The list of participants is long. The list of women involved in bringing this into being is longer. The list of reasons I felt utterly inadequate, longer still.

However, after brief chats with my husband, my cousin (a flower diva in her own right), and the Man Upstairs, I was in. Then I went to the orientation meeting. I was in all right, in over my head.

The slides we were shown of past participants' pieces were glorious, brilliant, clever, exquisite, creative—in other words, totally intimidating. As I trembled in the dark of the auditorium, my cousin, the diva, patted my hand and said casually, "You'll be fine." *Hmmm...*

I learned that I was to depict Corot's *Nymphes et Faunes*. I had some ideas. Mainly, I knew I wanted to use a mirror to represent the stream in this lovely landscape, and I wanted somehow to have Debussy's "Prelude to the Afternoon of a Faun" playing alongside my flowers.

From conception to birth was a whole 'nother column. Suffice it to say that I had to do something universally repugnant—I had to ask for help—every step of the way, from my husband, a MacGyver type whose motto is, "Don't spend money on that; I can make one," to the adolescent computer nerd genius guy at the Apple store.

But it got done. And it all worked. Sort of.

A good friend helped me assemble the assemblage the day of the installation. (I could never have wrapped that vine around my iPod cord like she did—my hands were shaking too badly.)

When all was done, we packed up and cleaned up, and went

about the all-important task of snooping around to see what everyone else was up to. I was dazzled, and stimulated. All that creativity swirling around in one building was downright energizing.

My husband and I returned that night for the Preview Party. Party I did not. I was too preoccupied with whether people were able to make the iPod work on my "work."

Apparently they succeeded, as did many others throughout the exhibit. By Saturday morning (two days after the Preview Party) the battery was dead, and the leaf camouflaging the iPod was singed and smelly. (Note to self: Bring adolescent computer nerd genius guy from Apple store next time.)

I did receive numerous compliments and pats on the back from the flower "powers that be"—and all in all felt honored, humbled, and somewhat bemused that a girl, who never put jonquils in a jelly jar before 2003, had a piece in a gallery next to a Camille Corot. ⁂

Rowdy groomsmen topple Rose Bush's topiaries in

french fried

ONCE, IN AN APARTMENT FAR, FAR AWAY—Lausanne, Switzerland, to be precise—I was introduced to Francophilia, believe it or not. My father, who moved us there for business reasons, was determined that, since we were a stone's throw away from the great source of so many things wonderful and beautiful (i.e., France), we would be exposed to and educated to appreciate these "things."

It worked. My brother and I, young sponges that we were, picked up French, albeit with a slight sing-songy lilt that is common in the Canton de Vaud. (We would later be mocked and ridiculed mercilessly in our adult travels to France by snooty *garçons*.)

We also picked up a love of art (*Winged Victory of Samothrace*—much more impressive than that stodgy old *Mona Lisa* who had been so built up by our parents), music (Sylvie Vartan, Françoise Hardy, and Johnny Hallyday), and of course the ubiquitous gourmet fare. Though I much preferred the *tartine et chocolat* to the *trout meunière*, and still do.

When we returned to our native Alabama a few years after we'd left, my mother, in an attempt to replicate our Swiss/French environment, covered my bedroom in blue toile and forced me to speak French to her, even in front of my friends—which was utterly degrading and humiliating for a nine-year-old. They all thought I was a terrible show-off.

Though having experienced a few French traumas, I found myself drawn to the language, customs, and style throughout high school, college, and the rest. So, it seemed natural when asked to do the flowers and décor for my goddaughter's nuptials that I should cull from the aesthetic I was weaned on.

First and foremost, there would be topiaries, numerous topiaries. A vestige of Versailles was the feel I was going for. After diligent searching via phone and visits to area nurseries, I came up with seven. Clearly, I would have to explore other allées. I called my landscaper, a can-do guy if I ever met one.

"Sure, no sweat. How many you need?" was his reply.

I had calculated that in order to turn the wedding reception into the vision of Versailles I longed for, I'd need at least 50 large topiaries. Single-ball and double-ball junipers, gardenias, and yellow-gold lantanas. Perfect. I knew I could sell them once the wedding was over.

All went well with the design. I planned to recapitulate the round forms in all the floral arrangements using shades of merlot, marigold, hot green, yellow, and apricot. I also repeated the round forms, somewhat, in pluots, nectarines, and lemons carefully mounded at each topiary's base—a lovely French flourish à la Christian Tortu.

That is, until the young groomsmen and their friends, after a few glasses of Champagne, began eyeing the fruit with mischievous intent.

The next thing I knew, fruit fights to rival *Animal House* and much juggling ensued. (Someone later asked the mother of the bride if she paid extra for the jugglers.) I even heard that a neighborhood pooch found great relief on one of the outside topiaries. All-purpose topes.

The wedding was a huge success, and a good time was had by all. But meanwhile, if anyone should like to purchase a topiary at a greatly reduced price, please contact me through the *Flower* website. My house and garden are looking decidedly French, which I would love, ordinarily, but it's a shingle, Dutch farmhouse. ❧

Flower magazine launches in Atlanta, despite a freak accident on I-85 in

almost gone with the wind

WOE BE UNTO YOU when you think you have all your peonies in place. I had dotted every i and crossed every t concerning the March 21ˢᵗ *Flower* magazine launch party at the Atlanta Botanical Garden and was feeling pretty confident when, around lunchtime, I arrived to survey the space and heard those words that, though meant to comfort, strike fear and dread into the heart of a hostess/wife: "Your husband called, and he's fine, but there's been a little accident."

Many of you may recall my MacGyver-like husband from the first Not So Prim Rose column. Well, in this scenario his talents were put to use bringing 10 wooden pedestals to Atlanta from Birmingham in a recycled rental trailer that had definitely seen better days.

He was almost home free when, to hear him tell it, he had exited I-20 onto I-85, around the curving ramp, and was sailing into Atlanta when he heard a loud crash, looked in the rearview mirror, and scarily, saw nothing. Then, all at once, he witnessed sparks flying, cars swerving, the detached trailer careening through lanes of traffic, landing on the other shoulder, wobbling, and coming to a standstill. All the while, my MacGyver focused on slowing down, praying hard, helpless to affect the outcome.

Miraculously, not one car or truck was struck by the projectile trailer. But that still left the problem of how to get the pedestals to the party. Our intrepid purveyor simply pulled onto the shoulder of the exit and proceeded to reverse to the point of ejection. He then jumped out of his truck and began to portage the pedestals one by one from the trailer (which at this point was smoking and minus one wheel) into his truck. Six fit in the back, and the last four were strapped to the roof in true MacGyver fashion with a bungee cord and a few dog leashes. At which point, he slowly proceeded to the venue, where he was met by me and all the floral designs that were waiting to perch on the plinths.

Hours later, after a hot shower and much head shaking and recounting of the incident, we arrived at the garden and proceeded to enjoy a splendid launch party, complete with sumptuous food, marvelous company, and exquisite flowers.

I think it was all the sweeter in view of the averted disaster. This flower business is an adventure, to say the least, and I wouldn't have it any other way. Next stop was Nashville, where we used indigenous pedestals. ❧

An Easter weekend wedding party feels more like Christmas in

bad friday

AS I PEN THIS PIECE, I will be preparing to attend a wedding in the mountains of North Carolina. Ahhh, relief from Alabama's punishing Indian summer. Though I look forward to the cool breezes of October in the Smokies, a mere five months ago I would have welcomed the swelter.

My husband and I and 12 other couples gave an engagement party at our house to celebrate the upcoming mountain nuptials. We thought Friday, April 6th, would be the perfect date, as many would be home for Easter that weekend, and the weather would most likely be temperate. We were half right.

The theme for the evening was rustic and informal—mountain mojitos in Mason jars, dining tables sporting burlap tablecloths, "field" flowers lovingly arranged in larger Mason jars on each table, hurricane lamps, even a trio of bluegrass-y musicians, the "Ishkooda Ramblers"—all to be set up on the lawn.

Throughout the week leading up to the event, I'd been hearing gentle caveats from cohostesses that a cold snap was in the forecast. Each time, I threw my head back and laughed saying, "Those guys are never right!" or "Yeah? Well, that's why they make blue jean jackets."

I did concede to allow the hostesses to deliver two fire pits. *I'll humor 'em,* I thought to myself.

Fast-forward to the afternoon of the party: lovely, sunny, a little breezy. Tables, cloths, flowers, jars, and lanterns were all delivered.

We began to set up. My first indication that I had perhaps misjudged the accuracy of the forecast came when the Mason jars full of flowers and water kept tumping over. My wonderful, practical sister-in-law suggested putting glass rocks in the bottoms of the jars. We poured every glass rock we could purchase from a nearby floral retailer into the jars and then stood back to admire our genius. Immediately a strong gust knocked EVERY jar over again.

Hmmm. I won't quote the expletives that were hurled, but suffice it to say, we were miffed. The only other solution was to remove the flowers until party time—which we did. Party time arrived and my husband came in the kitchen to ask if I'd like him to light a fire.

"Why would we need a fire, when it's not cold!?" I snapped. As he walked away, I could hear him murmuring under his breath something about my being in weather denial. I then peered through the french doors—now closed up tight—and witnessed, with a sigh, the first group of guests approaching in jackets, sweaters, pashminas, under down vests, even a hooded ski jacket. And it was only going to get colder as the sun went down.

Now, I'm as game as the next gal, but we were expecting 130, and our house, although quaint and just right for us, holds about 75, and that's pushing it.

Things started out OK, with lots of young people outside listening to the Ramblers. I noticed right away, however, the majority of them huddled around the fire pits.

These kids are lightweights, I observed to myself. I'll start a movement with some of the older, heartier menfolk. A few faithful friends complied, but once I turned my back, they were right back inside, in front of the fire, drinking mountain mojitos.

By mid-party, there was not one square inch of space to be had in the house. Even the Ramblers gave up and came in from the cold. But somehow, no one cared. I looked around and realized the closeness had created a sort of playful, silly atmosphere that allowed (forced) people to engage with whoever was next to them. It was wall-to-wall people, wall-to-wall gaiety, late into the night—a huge, serendipitous success.

My only regret was, of course, that the flowers got such short shrift. ✴

A directionally challenged Rose Bush roams the French countryside in

la vie en not so prim rose

I HAD A WHOLE DIFFERENT "ROSE" PLANNED, and then I went to Provence. One of my all-time favorite books about France is Peter Mayle's *A Year in Provence*. I remember my husband having a scare years ago, as he came down to the beach and saw me from behind, my head thrown back, shoulders jerking up and down—he was sure I was having some kind of seizure. In reality I was seized with paroxysms of laughter, as I read Peter's account of *les gens du Luberon*. I couldn't wait!

My "Tour de France" began with a mapquest from Marseille to Bonnieux. First of all, let me recommend not doing that—mainly because the Marseille airport is not in Marseille. I ended up going an hour and a half in the wrong direction to get to the first instruction on mapquest, during which time I stopped in traffic and asked a garbageman directions. Though I am semi-fluent in French, the only word I understood was "McDonald's."

Now, there's a uniquely European way of driving that, though initially unnerving in its seemingly utter disregard for other cars, strangely, kind of works. It took me a few heart-stopping near misses to surrender to the organized chaos of this dance. Once I calmed down enough to proceed, it became abundantly clear that the tangle of signs appearing at random intervals were no help. There was not a street sign to be found among 'em. I began to pray.

Next, I spotted a random sign that mentioned something familiar: Aix en Provence. I remembered that Bonnieux was in that general direction, so I went thataway.

Finally out of Marseille, I breathed a sigh of relief. *I'm on my way now.* But as my late father-in-law was fond of saying, "There's many a slip between the cup and the lip." Though the natives know their land very well, and know exactly what they mean by *la colline la-bas, en droite, vers le bâtiment brun* (the hill over there, on the right, near the brown building), there are lots of hills over there on the right, and plenty of brown buildings.

I venture to say that between my initial discovery of the road to Aix and arriving at my destination, I must have gone down eight to 10 wrong roads and stopped almost as many times to ask directions. At one point, I was sure there was a plot perpetrated by locals to keep tourists from finding their way.

Just when I was close to camping out in my rental Renault on the side of the road, I spied a *station de service*. With the cynicism of a weary and beleaguered traveler, I turned in, thinking, *What the heck, I'll give it one more shot*—when what should I spy by the entrance of the station but a huge display of FLOWERS!!!—all kinds, all colors, all shapes, all wrapped in the white butcher paper of the street vendor, all saying, "It's OK, don't worry, we're here, you know us, you're on the right track."

As I asked yet again for directions, I heard those words I'd been longing to hear: *"C'est juste la-bas, un tourne et voilà."* (It's just over there, one turn and you're there.) And it was and I am. ❧

Rose Bush's treacherous
trip home starts with a bang
and ends with a fall in

a hunting I did go and barely did make it back

"HONEY, I CAN'T POSSIBLY go to Mississippi in mid-December for two days on a hunting trip. A) It's mid-Christmas season and all that that implies. B) I've got flowerin' to do. C) I don't hunt."

But I did go, and it was sublime.

We weren't holed up in a cabin with no amenities in the middle of nowhere. We were wined, dined, and generally spoiled rotten in an antebellum home-cum-hunting club, in the middle of nowhere. Midway through the two days, I began to think maybe I could get used to this kind of hunting. I was even looking through Orvis catalogues on the sly before breakfast.

Though I had brought lots of *Flower* work along, I didn't really think I'd have much time to devote. But somehow, I managed to complete two projects and still go along for the ride on a morning hunt. As we were pulling out of the driveway to return home, I smiled at my husband and told him that it had been a perfect trip. He concurred, and we rode along in the afterglow of a successful expedition.

Just outside of Eutaw, Alabama, however, smoke began to shroud our SUV, lights started flashing, and my beloved whipped off the highway and quickly cut the engine. I looked at the dash and EVERY graphic was lit up, including one I'd never seen, of a car with all the doors open—which said to me: "GET OUT! GET OUT NOW!"

So we did.

But once the car was off, the smoke died down. We got back in and called a towing company—an hour and a half away. While we waited, I worked and the great sportsman next to me slept.

Finally, after dark, a huge truck pulled up to save the day and drove our vehicle up onto the bed, dog box on the back and all. (I kept asking if the dogs could ride in the cab with us, to no avail.)

But we made good time and enjoyed visiting with our tow-truck driver, Johnnie, hearing all about what his 9-year-old little girl wanted for Christmas, and talking about football and the like.

We were all smiles and conviviality as we approached the last mile of our trip, when the truck began coughing and sputtering. I didn't say a word. I just sat and watched as the unthinkable happened: The tow truck ran out of gas. There in four-lane traffic by the biggest mall in Birmingham, we sat shaking our heads and laughing.

Johnnie called his office, and they sent help in the form of a little bitty tow truck and a rope—and three guys who reminded me of nothing so much as Larry, Darryl, and his other brother Darryl. Their plan was to use the rope to tow the big truck with the SUV and dog box on it up to the gas station. We had other ideas and talked them into actually going to said station and purchasing gas and coming back with it.

Once we were on our way again, we all laughed and agreed that this would be one for the books (or magazine in my case). Johnnie took us home before dropping our truck at the shop, for which we were most grateful.

After he backed up our driveway to expedite unloading the dogs and luggage, I thanked him, wished him a Merry Christmas, opened the door of the truck, and—forgetting that I was higher off the ground than usual—fell five feet to the ground, rolled a few feet, and lay there facedown thinking, *I am NEVER going ANYWHERE with my husband AGAIN!*

But suddenly, as I realized I was lying on the soft, welcoming carpet of zoisia, I burst out laughing and thought to myself, *Well, I could have landed in the rose garden.* ❧

Rose Bush attends
a wedding for better
and worse in

wedding bell blues

ONE OF THE MANY CHALLENGES in life is punctuality. I think one reason I'm perpetually five or 10 minutes late to everything is that everything always takes longer than I think it will. This truth was driven home to me in my days as a flower-shop girl. We would plan the day's work schedule for a wedding, say, and allot one hour to put up sprays on sconces at the reception, and sure enough, forget the wire and have to drive back to the shop. Presto! One hour, transformed into three.

So, in preparing to attend the first wedding of spring in my burg, I was determined to "get me to the church on time." To be sure, I checked my laptop calendar: wedding at six at a downtown cathedral.

My daughter and I arrived at 5:15, deliriously happy to have a parking place right by the church and patting ourselves on the back about the great seats we were sure to secure. We leisurely crossed the street and greeted a bridesmaid, seven or eight groomsmen, and the mother of the bride—none of whom seemed overly impressed at our early arrival. As we walked up the steps and into the church, I had a sinking feeling. *Wait a minute, this is too good to be true.*

The church was full of people—none of whom looked dressed for a six o'clock wedding. Furthermore, there was a service in progress. I thought to myself, *Well, they better hurry up in there if this wedding's going to start on time.*

Heading back outside, I stage-whispered to the bridesmaid, "You know there's a service going on? Wait a minute. What time is the wedding?!"

She sheepishly held up seven fingers. I could feel my face flush as my daughter and I had to run the gamut of wedding people back to our car. We went all the way home and came back an hour later.

Surprise! Not a parking place in sight. By the time we got

inside, the only seats available were smack-dab behind a massive column. Though a lovely and no doubt structurally necessary architectural detail, it obscured the entire ceremony from our view.

As the recessional played, the heavens opened up. Most days in drought-ridden Birmingham I would welcome the sound of thunder. Not this day.

Sporting silk and no umbrella, I cringed at the sight of everyone else's bumbershoots opening up and the thought of my car, five city blocks away. I looked at my daughter, in her new daffodil-yellow dress with her hair and makeup perfect, and made a snap decision to let her wait against the side of the building under the eaves, while I ran, sploshing through puddles, to fetch the car.

We arrived at the reception just as the deluge ceased and agreed to split up so I could check out the flowers and she could find her friends. I smiled the proud mama smile as I watched her walk away, until I noticed a huge black swath of soot across the lower portion of her new daffodil-yellow dress. I lunged for her and asked her come to the powder room with me. (Only a mom can rub your backside with a wet cloth in the powder room in front of a bunch of strangers from Mississippi.)

Out in the world of the reception, I made my way through a wonderland of sumptuous flowers, jazzy music, and really fun wedding guests. I did not, however, make it to the food. On my way out, I spied a basket full of tulle-wrapped treats and grabbed one. Heading home, I unwrapped the bundle, tossed a Jordan almond into my mouth, and promptly cracked a filling.

I was just recovering from what I hoped was the last challenge of the evening when, walking in my front door and catching my reflection in the mirror, I had yet another jarring moment. Having been so consumed with "getting out damned spot" on my daughter's dress, I neglected to check my own look and had apparently spent the entire reception with rain-flattened hair and streaky makeup.

As I winced at the thought, I looked down, and crumpled in my hand was the card from the candy: "Five Jordan almonds for guests to eat, to remind us that life is both bitter and sweet."

Uh-huhhh... ⚜

Rose Bush's husband, MacGyver,
is dressed to impress in

black tie, white tie, no tie, oh my!

AS YOU MIGHT IMAGINE, being a *Flower* editor, I attend a lot of flowery events. Some could best be described as snazzy. I bend every effort to look my best, not draw any negative attention to myself, and generally come off as fairly comme il faut—and in the process catch up with the event photographer, planner, and floral designer, all the while assessing the floral component for reportage.

Generally, I attend these soirées alone, but lately I've been accompanied by my husband. (Many of you recall his MacGyver–ish adventures from earlier columns.) This addition has proved salutary, as he is remarkable on his feet, cuts quite a dash, and is able to lift heavy objects, such as my suitcases.

The last few events, however, have been marred (for me) by my inability to designate the proper attire for my "date." First, we traveled out of state to a ball, which I assumed, like many balls, was black tie. We waltzed through the entrance and made our way into the loggia of the old manse, and I immediately broke out into a cold sweat. Every gentleman there was sporting a decidedly non-black tie, i.e., white tie and tails. MacGyver didn't even notice. (Typical male—in a good way.)

Though I had charming dinner partners and was among the first to rush the stage when the talent came on, I spent the evening, by and large, feeling self-conscious for my husband— and by association, me. (I know; it's awful, but there it is.)

The second sartorial sabotaging occurred when we were set to attend a midsummer wedding in Alabama. It was a six o'clock wedding, which to me says black tie, right? My sweet husband this time had checked with a friend and fellow wedding guest he happened to run into the day of the wedding. "Eastlake says he's not wearing black tie. He doesn't think anyone is," my beloved informed me.

But I insisted on black tie and off we went. We parked and I looked in the side-mirror, and my heart sank as I watched waves of male guests make their way up the church steps in suits, coat and tie, and even NO TIE! I gave my lips a swipe of lipstick and said to my laughing, yet at this point somewhat chagrined husband, "You may be the only one in black tie, but you're right!"

Scant comfort it was. Another dread-filled entrance ensued as we strolled into the church in which all the men were non-formally attired. I wish I could say that I sat in reverent contemplation waiting for the ceremony to begin, but I'd be lying. I sat, distracted and self/husband-conscious. And this continued throughout the festivities.

I remember that the flowers at both events were fabulous, but don't ask me to be specific. I'll have to wait for the photographers' discs.

Meanwhile, my MacGyver's next adventure is to wrest all invitations away from me so that *he* can decide what to wear. ⊰

Rose Bush narrowly escapes a demonstration disaster in *midnight at the oasis*

"I'M TOO OLD FOR THIS," I groused to my husband on the phone, tucked into my hotel room for the night.

After having driven eight hours and schlepped buckets of flowers and greenery, a toolbox, bags of green Oasis floral-foam spheres, magazine posters, easels, and suitcases along with me, I was duly pooped when I arrived in a new town earlier that night for a floral convention the next day.

However, I had been quickly revived as I witnessed a police car, siren blaring, blue lights flashing, wheeling into the porte-cochère. As the cruiser sped down the lot in pursuit of the alleged perpetrator, I emerged from my car and proceeded to the check-in counter.

I asked the receptionist what was up, and he casually replied that someone had just been held up at gunpoint in the back parking lot. He then shared that this had never happened before. (What about that statement was supposed to be comforting?) I knew I should've brought my husband, or at least my pepper spray. All I was packing in the way of self-defense were some prickly grasses and a really big pocketbook.

It took two trips to get all the items out of my car, and in view of the proximity of the crime scene, I made haste. I never stopped to ask any details about the convention, just checked in and went straight to my room. After an hour of unloading all my goods into the room and telephoning my husband to regale him with the events of the evening, I began to map out my presentation, scheduled for first thing the next morning.

My plan was to use plant material that was all locally grown or organic (or both) and recycled containers for my demonstration. Having scored several bunches of sunflowers, I decided to be really modern and edgy and pull all their petals off, stick the eyes in Oasis spheres, and then place them atop big mercury-glass containers.

Without extra buckets, I had to soak the Oasis in my bathtub. I was just putting the last globe in the tub and squinching fountain grass, okra, and other "green" greenery onto the counter when a convention representative called, reminding me of the welcome reception. OK...

I've shared bathrooms with roommates (many), children (three), and husbands (two), but I've never had to compete for the mirror with poke salad. After a quick turn around the party, I raced back up to my room-cum-flower shop. I still had my sunflower spheres to do and lots of dividing of grasses and flowers. Grabbing my snips, I began to behead the sunflowers and de-petal them. All were neatly laid out on a towel in my room as I lifted the first Oasis sphere out of the tub (which, of course, by this time was filled with green water and multiple bobbing balls).

I began poking the short stems into the Oasis, and just as I would poke the next one in, the one before would fall out. (Note to self: Always do a dry run before a demo/presentation.)

So, I had now cut the heads off several bunches of organic sunflowers and soaked numerous Oasis balls, only to be able to use neither. The only other flowers I could have used were zinnias, but their stems were too soft. Lacking any picks, I decided to punt the whole cool globe concept.

This meant I was effectively done for the evening, as the remaining plant material was all to be used in my demo the following day. Bright and early the next morning, I began to run my shower, only to realize I had to dispose of the soaked, now 10-pound Oasis balls. Ughhh. So I picked up the phone and bellowed, "HOUSEKEEPING!!!!!"

This was turning into a real logistical nightmare. After getting dressed and loading all my flowers back onto a luggage cart, I wheeled down to the lobby to locate the venue for my presentation. A half-mile later inside the convention center, I found my space. I steered straight for it and started to turn in, when what should I spy directly across the hall but a HUGE flower-filled room equipped with tables, buckets, sinks—you get the picture—and all the other presenters working on their designs.

I may have missed this particular piece of information in my haste the night before, but I did manage to avoid the night bandit, pull together a presentation, and determine to use the buddy system for future travels. ⚘

A trip to New York
turns a little too hip in

heartbreak hotel

WHILE STEPPING OUT OF THE CAB from the airport one evening in New York City, and looking forward to the sanctuary of the posh hotel before me, my dreams were dashed by techno music blaring from hidden speakers—meant, I'm sure, to impart a cool, sophisticated vibe to arriving guests. But to me, a travel weary, middle-aged *Flower* gal, it imparted, "What are *you* doing here? This place is for scenesters and celebrities!"

As I tried desperately to identify the doorman from among a scrum of black-clad street dudes, the cab driver took pity on me and signaled one of said dudes to help with my bags. (How he was able to pick out the hotel employee is beyond me.) I thanked him with the first bill I could find in my wallet and proceeded warily and shakily into a lobby that reminded me of the bar scene in the first *Star Wars* movie.

Next challenge: to locate/identify the registration desk. Though there were several really sleek, modern surfaces in this area, all with polished chrome bowls filled with polished Granny Smith apples, not a one of them possessed the requisite polished person to check me in.

As I stood in this vortex of futuristic isolation, I prayed quietly for help, *I need somebody,* then crazily giggled to myself imagining the Lennon/McCartney scenario that prompted those lyrics. On the heels of this sacred moment, a gentleman appeared behind one of the sleek surfaces, staring at me in mild amusement. "Welcome to the Z Hotel. Checking in?"

After successfully accomplishing that mission, I endeavored to locate the elevators. They, like everything else, were discreet and (to these eyes) unrecognizable. I stood and waited for other guests who looked like they might be "going up" and promptly followed them as the cave-like Aladdin's doors opened. Aha! They used their room key to get to their floor, but strangely, after they disembarked, my key did not grant the magical access I was by this time SO longing for.

Struggling to tune out the ubiquitous techno strains and figure out the secret motion that would get me to the Shangri-la of my room and bed, I found myself grumbling to myself, as I had on several other *Flower* escapades, "I'm too old for this."

Finally, after holding my mouth just right and clicking my heels together three times, I was mercifully delivered to my floor, room, and bed. Things were looking up, until I tried in vain to turn off the clock radio. Though tuned to a much more soothing classical station, I still needed—no, craved—silence.

To avoid tearing the clock out of the wall, I did what any middle-aged parent of a 20-something would do in this situation: I telephoned my daughter for technical support. She lovingly helped me navigate the buttons with hardly a chuckle and offered to help me figure out the mini-bar. I responded that I somehow always managed to access the cache of chocolates and nut mixes in the "bar" (unfortunately), but thanked her very much.

The next day, after a good night's sleep, I considered that I might have a smoother time of it in the "brave new world" of my hotel, but I was mistaken. I could not access the fitness room (not due to any technical difficulty, but rather an early-morning, rush-hour mob scene, unlike anything I had ever seen.) So I returned to my room, busted a few Pilates moves on the paper-thin commercial carpet, showered, dressed, packed, called an old favorite hotel, and booked a room for the rest of my stay.

Sailing out of the space odyssey lodgings, I glimpsed a blur of color in the niches of the bar. Ever the flower fanatic, I turned back—and there, in a perfect twist of irony, sat the most exquisite floral designs I'd seen in a long time. I asked the doorman to hold my cab while I found the nearest polished person and promptly ascertained the name of their florist. ❧

Rose Bush and the *Flower* girls encounter rats, cats, and rascals in

animal house work

ONLY LOCAL *FLOWER* READERS are aware of the fact that our office is located in my guesthouse. We call it the "International Headquarters" of *Flower* magazine. More humorous when we first launched, we are now actually on newsstands in 18 countries. Meanwhile, we remain in the "IHQ."

Though this affords a great savings in overhead and lends a casual-Friday feel to every day, it has its drawbacks. Ordinarily, these little foxes nibble at the vines only on occasion. Yesterday, the whole vineyard came down.

In my line of work, I travel a good bit, attending and speaking at floral and garden events. One day on my return from the road, I was greeted by my daughter, who had arrived home for a visit. Heading to her room in the guesthouse (over the IHQ), she promptly fled back downstairs into the office hollering that there was some disgusting smell in her room.

After a collective sigh (and thinking she was a bit of a princess), we *Flower* girls strode upstairs to get to the bottom of things. On entering, we were assaulted by the horrible odor of a dead animal—at which point, screaming *Flower* girls stampeded back down the stairs.

Our hero, David of Athena Pest Control (named by the owners of the company after the Greek goddess of war, because they realize it's an ongoing battle), had set traps, and one had apparently worked. In response to our call, David arrived on the scene and was given a standing ovation by everyone as he very efficiently and somewhat proudly carried out the pest in a garbage bag and, with it, the awful odor.

Back to work we went, sure that the worst of our animal troubles were over. Not so. Our managing editor, due to the somewhat relaxed environment in the IHQ, had taken to periodically bringing her rescue kitten to work. Usually this was not a problem, and on this particular day, said kitty had been left at home. However, my daughter's kitty had also made the trip home and didn't much care for the scent of the other woman.

We know this, because when we all got back from lunch, we experienced yet another unpleasant animal odor: Visiting kitty had apparently picked up the other feline fragrance from the managing editor's computer bag and proceeded to display her displeasure in that uniquely charming way cats have—she tee-teed all up in that bag. Lovely.

I mentioned that I'd love to stay and help clean up, but remembered I had to go cover a very important flower show and beat a hasty retreat.

The show was fabulous, and many there had seen the magazine and subscribed. *Maybe this won't be such a bad day after all,* I thought to myself. As I drove back to the IHQ, I reminisced with a warm glow about the past few days of travel, which had consisted of fabulous floral parties and events filled with fun, creative people, amazing flowers and gardens, and warm receptions.

As I exited my car back at the office, I was still thinking along overly confident lines: *Life is good! We're in high cotton now! This is the stuff! Wow, I can't believe how far we've come! How great is this!*

Right then and there, I was suddenly and rather harshly brought down to earth. As I unloaded my accoutrements right in front of the IHQ, with *Flower* girls gazing out the window at the scene, my husband's bird dog proceeded to casually lift his leg on my *Flower* bag, turn, and lope off after yet another enticing target. He was obviously not as impressed with me or the magazine as I was.

We have been soft-searching for just the right office space for about a year now, but in light of these recent incidents, it looks like we may escalate our efforts. ✂

Rose Bush relates
her travel trials and
tribulations in

ramblin' woes

AS I'VE MENTIONED BEFORE, travel is a big part of my life as a *Flower* editor. Since 9/11, travel in general has become more or less a case of, "How bad do you want to go?"

Some of my peregrinations pass more or less without incident—others, not so much. This account deals with two back-to-back trips (never a good idea) that went awry. I am unable to blame either incident on terrorists.

First, I was headed on a Sunday afternoon to New Orleans via Southwest Airlines (one of my favorites due to their democratic seating and the zany, cornball, Southern humor of their pilots and flight attendants). I sat at my gate (or so I thought) and settled in for a 45-minute wait during which I delved into the newest *Vogue*. Suddenly, I realized my flight was really late, but they hadn't made any announcements. And no one at the gate seemed particularly concerned.

I got up and went to the attendant, at which point I learned with horror that I was at the wrong gate and my flight had departed. Of course, there were no more flights to be had that night. So, I did what any *Flower* gal who was slated to be on TV at 6 a.m. in NOLA the next day would do—I hopped in my car and drove.

The trip was lovely, and I arrived without incident and slept for a whole three hours. When I got to the station and shared the story of my travel fiasco, the anchor of the morning show just laughed and said, "We could've filled that three minutes, no problem. You should have called."

What!? I'm expendable, replaceable; the show could have gone on without me!? Apparently. But I went on and pulled together a quick design, spread *Flower* magazine love and advice, and left.

With no rest for the weary, the very next morning my trusty assistant and I had to drive to Atlanta for a garden club appearance. Only a two-hour drive, no sweat. NOT.

Evidently, the much-prayed-for rains had finally come to

Georgia and flooded the entire area from 40 miles out of Atlanta, through the city, and out the other side. What was usually two hours quickly became five. My trusty (24-year-old) assistant had maps and apps all over her Blackberry and set about finding alternate routes for us.

Sadly, what often happened was we would sneakily take a turn and think, *Aha! We're free at last!*, only to find bumper-to-bumper traffic or road blocks where bridges or roads were washed out and not showing up on her apps and maps.

Meanwhile, T.A. (my trusty assistant) was texting the ladies in the garden club with updates, thinking they would say, "Oh, just turn around and go back; this is too much; you'll be too late." But no. These were garden-loving women who had gathered, cooked, and decorated and were going to wait out the vicissitudes of our travel and even find people to pick up their children at noon—all to hear about *Flower* and glean a few design tips. God love 'em.

We finally rolled in as the meeting was set to end. As we rushed in with our flowers and containers, the women welcomed us with enthusiasm and gratitude, incredulous that we had arrived. I proceeded to speak and demo with more humor and enthusiasm than ever before, I think, due to the thrill and flush of coming through yet another traveling trial.

We drove back pretty much the way we came (it took exactly another five hours, maps and apps included—but at least we gained an hour coming back) and pulled up to the IHQ. We were greeted by staffers wondering what took us so long—to which we responded, "How much time do you have?" ❧

A car trip without coolant turns into a hot mess in

ramblin' woes part 2

IT MUST SEEM BY NOW to readers that I am the world's worst traveler. It's entirely possible. When I finished my last installment, I thought I'd have to cast about for a new topic for the next column. *Surely no more "bad trips."* Wrong.

Recently, T.A. (my trusty assistant) and I drove to Huntsville,

Alabama, for a *Flower* event. We left Birmingham bright and early and were making good time, so I was reluctant to stop when my coolant level light flashed on. I called my husband, whom you know as "MacGyver," and asked if I could make it. "Sure, honey. Just stop at a fillin' station after the show and get some coolant."

All went well in the Rocket City, and we got back on the road at a more rapid speed than usual, as T.A. had a bachelorette party in Atlanta to attend. We were flying down I-65 when, all of a sudden, the steering wheel would barely turn, the screen started flashing, and a terrible smell filled the air.

"OH #@$*%!"

Of course, I had neglected to stop and get coolant, and just north of Cullman, Alabama, my car went on strike. I pulled over slowly into the "V" between the interstate and a merging lane, scared I couldn't make it all the way across the next lane to the shoulder. So, off the road but in the tiniest patch of grass imaginable, with semis, pickups, and cars blowin' by us on both sides like we were at the Talladega 500 or something, I got out with my bottle of Dasani and popped the hood. I thought I'd just pour a little water in there and fix 'er right up. Wrong again.

So I called Roadside Assistance (or should I say "Roadside Resistance"). I read the VIN number to the woman on the other end, and she came back with, "I'm sorry, but your car's no longer under warranty." *OK, I guess I'll just stay here then...*

"Well," I responded calmly, "that's OK; I'll pay for the wrecker." "What is your location?" the voice on the other end said. I told her, to which she responded, "Are you sure?"

And it deteriorated from there. The last helpful response she gave consisted of, "We can't find a wrecker near Cullman; we'll have to send one from Birmingham. He'll be there in about an hour and a half. Oh, yes, and he doesn't take credit cards or checks, but he said he'd be glad to run you by an ATM machine."

I curtly responded, "Thanks. We'll handle it from here." T.A. and the managing editor, back at the International Headquarters, joined forces. M.E. Googled Cullman wrecker services, T.A. made the call, and Presto! Fifteen minutes later, up roared Steve, originally from Spearfish, South Dakota, with his wrecker and double cab, a lovely attitude, and "Yes, ma'am, I take American Express."

The next thing I knew, I was snug in the back seat of the wrecker and headed home, my cute little car with the *Flower* magazine license plate staring me in the face in the rear window. Thinking I'd escaped unscathed, I found out T.A. had taken a picture with her phone of the car in tow and sent it out with color commentary on Twitter and Facebook.

Ah, the double-edged sword of technology— helped and humiliated all in the span of a half hour. ⚜

Rose Bush learns the importance of research in

rose of sharon joad

DESPITE THE MANY MISHAPS recorded in previous stories, I continue to travel and represent *Flower* magazine. However, it's one thing for your car to break down in a small town and quite another to show your you-know-what in a big city in front of a lot of bigwigs. The phone call that precipitated my latest comeuppance: "Ms. Bush, we would love for you to speak at our antiques show. The last speaker was Renny Reynolds, and before that, P. Allen Smith." *WHOA*.

"What do you think your topic might be?" Rather than get back to her later, I felt compelled to come with a response: "How 'bout antique roses and roses in antiques?" "Perfect!" the caller exclaimed. *HELP*.

Now, I know a little bit about roses, enough to be dangerous. But having studied art history in college and wintered at Winterthur Museum, I thought, *Well, at least the antique part's in the bag.* I got started right away and did what any middle-aged dabbler would do; I commissioned an intern to do the research. Every day for weeks the IHQ looked like an all-nighter in a college dorm—with books and legal pads and laptops spread hither and yon.

Plus, I called local and regional experts, interviewed the premier rosarian in my neck of the woods, and read all the notes compiled by our intern. I even listened to Sting's version of a medieval Christmas carol, "There is No Rose of Such Virtue," to get into the spirit.

The intern put together a flawless PowerPoint comprised of rose history and past *Flower* magazine articles on roses, as well as some choice images of well-documented antiques bearing rose motifs. The last component of my presentation was to be a demonstration of the ever-popular French hand-tied bouquet using antique roses, of course. And I had cleverly chosen an antique silver vessel as container for said hand-tied.

The presentation went smoothly. I miraculously kept all the

rose facts and names and such straight during the PowerPoint, and I sailed through the roses in antiques part, as well as the demo. I crowned the presentation with a quick reference to the provenance of my antique container, took a bow, and exited the stage, fairly glowing with a mix of self-satisfaction and relief. Not so fast.

As I began my tour of the antiques show, my first stop was a booth purveying antique silver. I graciously admired the dealer's wares and suddenly spotted the exact same style container that I had used.

"Oh, I see you have the same tea caddy I used in my demonstration!" I exclaimed. "Ahem. Actually," the dealer commented, "that's a biscuit box. Several women came in after your presentation and checked with me."

Aaarrrgggghhhhh.

In researching rose terms in preparation for my presentation, I had come across an old familiar character from *The Grapes of Wrath*, Rose of Sharon Joad. The description I read of her? "Full of self-importance and false confidence."

Ouch. ⚜

A long day runs the
gamut between nobility
and hairballs in

royal pains

IN CASE YOU, DEAR READER, are laboring under the misconception that my life is a bed of roses—perhaps say, those few who've not followed my peregrinations and humiliations in this column—allow me to disabuse you of that notion as I chronicle a day in the life of Rose Bush: Monday, June 14th, 2010.

I rise at 3 a.m. in order to have coffee and go over my notes in preparation for a 4 a.m. phone interview with a duchess, who lives in the U.K. (I wish you could have seen all the *Flower* girls the Friday before, Googling "how to address a duchess" so that I didn't start off with a faux pas.) The hour-long conversation is delightful, but then I'm too stimulated to go back to sleep. I press on through the morning in a bit of a fog—finding myself lapsing into a slight British accent here and there.

Midafternoon, out in the *Flower* IHQ (my guesthouse), it's business as usual until our editorial assistant suddenly swoops over to whisk the printer off the top of a chest of drawers. I look up and realize she's saving it from certain drowning, as we have a leak. No rain, mind you, just a leak, emanating from the ceiling—just behind my desk. Awesome.

I call our air-conditioning contractor (on speed dial for this over-50 gal), and they send over Eugene—Eugene of the dear, meek monotone and sweet countenance, who matter-of-factly informs me that it doesn't look good.

Prepared for the worst, I pull out my checkbook, but Eugene is not through. Next, he asks for a garbage bag so that he can carry out the two rodents he's come across while investigating the leak. (Thank God for men.)

As Eugene attempts his exit, stage left, the big brown truck pulls up and blocks him in. (IT'S THE SUMMER ISSUE!) More chaos ensues as all the *Flower* girls try to avoid contact with the garbage bag and move boxes around to make room for more boxes, all the while squealing with a mix of disgust re: the rodents, and glee re: the magazine. At the end of this long, colorful day, I think, *Well, now I can relax with a hot soak and a good night's sleep.* But apparently not.

First of all, I walk into the house to discover that the bird dog/billy goat has torn up the box containing my new dress for a family wedding, hot off the brown truck with the magazines. *Never mind, I can go shopping in the basement.*

Next? I trudge up to my bathroom to soak and find not one, but two hairballs in my tub courtesy of my cat, Marigold. So I shower instead. I tumble into bed next to my husband (whom many of you know as MacGyver, but whom some of you also know as an Episcopal priest) and fall instantly into a deep and well-deserved slumber. A few hours later, I'm well into REM sleep, and the phone rings. It's the alarm company calling to inform us that someone has broken into my husband's church. I turn on the light and read until he returns two hours later.

As I thrash around, trying in vain to sleep, I notice the time: 4 a.m. I could call the duchess. I know she's up.

Hydrangeas take a hit during a *Flower* delivery in

isn't that special, delivery

ONE OF THE HIGHLIGHTS of working at *Flower* is the arrival of the new issue. Generally, this occurs midmorning, when a brown truck pulls up to the International Headquarters and a man with a dolly brings us our precious cargo. Most recently, however, this was not the case.

{ NOT SO PRIM ROSE }

Interestingly, our managing editor had no sooner prodded me for a new Not So Prim Rose than I received a phone call from Derrick the truck driver saying, "Ms. Bush, I've got your magazines. I'm down on the lane, but I'm in an 18-wheeler and can't get up your driveway. Can you come down and get the boxes?" *No, but I can send some young* Flower *girls with their SUVs.*

The much-anticipated magazine was the fall issue. It was September in Alabama and therefore 97 degrees and humid. Derrick, in his air-conditioned cab, definitely had the better end of this deal.

I went back to work and then promptly received a phone call from my trusty assistant, who said, "You'd better get down here. There's a problem." As I stomped out the door, I mentioned over my shoulder to our managing editor, "Stay tuned. I think we may have a 'Rose' in the works."

I arrived at the bottom of the driveway to spy the 18-wheeler lodged (actually more like stuck) at an angle across the lane—nose in the middle of my neighbor's driveway across the street. Apparently Derrick was unable to negotiate the Austin Powers 15-point turn that would have extricated him from the wrong driveway. Not only was he stuck, but in the process, he'd trenched my neighbor's yard and pulled down a few hydrangea bushes in the bargain.

But the BEST part was that my neighbor was idling in her driveway, waiting to get out. Not only had she witnessed the carnage, she was now trapped. After profuse apologies and much groveling, I helped Derrick back up, straighten up, and head down the lane so that my neighbor could exit.

That done, we began to unload the boxes and place them in the backs of the SUVs. Let me remind you, it's September in Alabama, and we were all immediately in need of showers and some ice-cold Co-Colas. Next, Derrick attempted to back up the lane to the main street.

"Hold on, I'll guide you," said I, with all the bravado of one who's trying to instill confidence when she is completely out of her depth. Not in possession of the requisite orange aircraft marshalling batons, I resorted to wild flailing and gesticulating in an effort to direct Derrick backwards to the main road and to freedom.

You know the rest. Every time I got him almost completely backed onto the road, a stream of cars would pull up and need to get past. Derrick, eyes rolling, would inch back down the lane and let them by. This went on for a good while, when finally he was able to fully back out onto the main road and hightail it. He left without a wave or a goodbye, just a roar of the engine and blue-gray diesel fumes hanging in the air. (Bless his heart. I know he was done.) I slogged back up to the IHQ with a few choice words in mind for the trucking company, but in possession of what I thought was most likely my next Prim Rose dispatch.

As I walked in and relayed the story to our managing editor, she smiled, shrugged, and said, "Well, unfortunately, you cannot say that no flowers were harmed in the delivery of this magazine."

Funny. ⋇

Rose Bush's vacation
goes from
relaxing to vexing in

tough break

THOUGH I TRAVEL A LOT for *Flower*, I rarely vacate or recreate. I don't usually take notice of this until I find myself repeating myself, misplacing things (i.e. wallet in the freezer, etc.), sitting in front of my laptop unable to recall why, and begging my husband to go to fabulous parties without me—all signs of a much-needed break.

The week between Christmas and New Year's Eve is historically pretty quiet in the *Flower* world, so I settled on that time to travel to a country inn north of Birmingham and enjoy time away with my husband. In hindsight, "enjoy" might be too strong a word.

A drive of only a few hours brought us to an idyllic spot that yielded sighs of pleasure—which quickly turned to sighs of exasperation. For starters, the innkeeper had us scheduled to arrive the next day. So the heat was not turned on, and we were experiencing what seemed like the coldest snap in state history, but by morning the icicles began to melt off my nose.

We started to warm up and settle in, and after a day of reading and relaxing, we began to prepare for a semi-swanky soirée at some friends' mountain house nearby. Though I'm not a huge stylista, I do like to come off as at least well groomed.

Plan thwarted. As I turned on the blow-dryer, I heard a crack like gunfire, and the whole room went dark. My husband, aka MacGyver, was unable to remedy the problem, as I had apparently done more damage than just a blown fuse. (Old houses can be so charming.) Luckily, we were the only guests in the inn, so we had our pick of rooms to move to later on.

But meanwhile, I arrived at the party sporting limp, damp, somewhat-frozen hair, and a bit of an attitude.

Our next fun surprise, once moved to our new room, was being awoken at 2 a.m. by a chirping smoke detector. You know the kind. They chirp, then stop, and you think it's over and are just drifting back to sleep when they chirp again.

We called security, and they sent over Otis, who basically helped my husband move a table so that he (my husband) could get on top of it and dismantle the smoke detector. (Thanks, Otis!) As you can imagine, after this adventure, we lay there, wide awake for hours, running the emotional gamut between furious and highly amused.

The last day of our relaxing getaway was relatively uneventful, which was a relief since I woke up with a sore throat, cough, and a fever of 101. At that point, I couldn't wait to get home and rest up from my vacation. ❧

Flower girls encounter serious car-tastrophes in

blooms off the roads

ONE THING I ALWAYS BRAG ABOUT is our crackerjack team of young *Flower* girls and how things run smooth as silk thanks to their Gen X, Y, and Z knowledge of new millennium technology, amazing attention to detail, and youthful exuberance.

I, on the other hand, need a drool nap every day around three o'clock and have trouble with the microwave. As vast as the chasm may be between us, there is one great equalizer: cars. We are all girls and, at the risk of offending the more feminist among us, all fairly helpless when faced with auto issues.

It was a brisk, bright February day in Alabama, and we were gearing up for a big floral and fashion event with one of our advertisers. All ducks were in their respective rows, and the team had mobilized to the venue—all except me.

Leaving from home to head to the event, I had forgotten my husband's caveat about the car being low on gas, but the gauge said I had 27 miles till empty. I think it was missing a decimal point, though, because no sooner had I crossed the highway one minute from home than the car began to sputter out. I managed to get off the road but was very glad no young *Flower* girls were within earshot as I hurled a few un-flowery words in the general direction of Bavaria.

When I calmed down, I called my trusty assistant. She came to pick me up, and we abandoned the vehicle on the side of the road.

The event was a triumph in every way. The Los Angeles fashion designer who'd flown in was delighted at the success of the show, as were our advertisers. The guests were reluctant to leave when the party was over (always a good sign) and ended up lingering on into the afternoon visiting and shopping. We *Flower* girls all stood around basking in our glory and then finally acknowledged we had to get back to work. "Let's get back to the office and tweet about our wonderful success!"

Floating along in that roseate glow of a job well done, one of our girls (the one in charge of the event) got into a rear-ender in the parking lot, and poof—the bubble burst, as her shiny new ride sustained a major bruise. Our *Flower* girl, of course, kept her cool and was a paragon of grace and poise.

Meanwhile, my trusty assistant and I bought gas, filled up my vehicle, and I was off—or not. The engine still wouldn't turn over. *What do you mean you can't leave your flashers on for seven hours without running down the battery?!?!* By this time I was ready to roll the car into the woods and leave it. But I did the next best thing. I abandoned it there AGAIN and caught a ride home with T.A.

The next day, as I prepared to commiserate with my fellow victim of car catastrophes, I learned that to boost her spirits, she had marched back into the store to treat herself to a little retail therapy. I smiled and thought, *Well hey, I got a shiny, new gas can out of the deal.* I'm always looking for the pony. ⚘

Rose Bush's
Southern hospitality
is put to the test in

pet peeve

MANY OF YOU MAY NOT BE AWARE that *Flower* has finally moved out of the International Headquarters (my guesthouse) into a for-real office—which is still a cozy cedar shake cottage, but larger and just down the road from the original office behind the Bush residence.

Phew! Now we can really spread out, get more work done, have everyone in one place, and be "pet free." (For the newer *Flower* reader, our office kitty and English Setter had made life a bit difficult and somewhat odiferous on occasion around the "home office.")

Happily ensconced in our new digs, one afternoon I received a call from one of our most distinguished and celebrated *Flower* friends. I leaned back leisurely in my new lumbar-supported office chair and began to converse with said bigwig when, all of a sudden, I saw a geyser-like movement out of the corner of my eye.

Without letting on that anything was amiss, I began to sweat profusely and listen to the caller rather half-heartedly as two neighborhood dogs continued to dig up our newly planted perennial bed, conveniently located just outside my window for my viewing pleasure. (The geyser-like movement was fast-moving dirt dug up and out into the newly mown yard.)

I wanted to laugh—or cry. I definitely wanted to beat on the window and stop the carnage, but I knew I was in that most unenviable of all places—utter helplessness. So I turned my full attention back to the still talking caller. When I finally got off the phone, I ran outside shooing the two agents of destruction off the property and then called the landscaper with my tale of woe.

A few canine-free weeks had passed, and it was the night of *Flower*'s party to celebrate the printing of the summer issue. I had planned and decorated the new *Flower* house to a fair thee well for her first fête, and the evening was in full swing when I noticed a huddle of *Flower* girls outside—leaning over, laughing, and petting something. Curious, I joined the group and promptly realized that the party had been crashed by none other than one of the "diggers."

"Isn't she cute!" exclaimed one *Flower* girl. "Look how she just lets you pet her! She's so sweet," sighed another. "And she's named after my favorite female vocalist!!" squealed a third, after eyeing her monogrammed collar.

Seething, and ready to haul "Stevie" to the pound—or at least not let her have any more hors d'oeuvres—I suddenly realized, *That dog was just being a dog. Dogs dig in the dirt, just like we do—they just don't let the perennials get in their way.*

What the heck, Stevie can stay. She's put a lot of sweat equity into the place. ❧

"Lights out" proves easier said than done for Rose Bush in *wild board*

IT SEEMS THE OLDER I GET, the more I'm bedeviled by technology. What I think happens is that the rate of my aging is in direct proportion to the warp speed of esoteric and Byzantine advancements in high-level gadgetry—which would not be a problem, except, in publishing, a girl's gotta keep up.

There are some days when I'm impressed with myself, like when I recently went to the Apple store, bought an iPad, and got home and was able to read *Flower* magazine on it. But then, the next day, I took it on a sales trip and forgot how to turn it on. (Yeah, there was no way I was calling the "Genius Bar" with that question.) I eventually figured it out but emerged even more wobbly than ever in this "brave new world."

The next challenge I faced was one of the sort that I would generally term a happy problem. It beset me in a fabulous hunting lodge where my husband and I were grateful houseguests over a Labor Day weekend. We were on a real getaway, enjoying the beauty, tranquility, and storied hospitality of the Eastern Shore of Maryland.

After our first dazzling day of tours, outdoor activities, and a delectable dinner, we were fairly giddy at the prospect of our cozy bed in the lodge, when we both realized we couldn't work the computer keypad that controlled all the lights in the house. *That's simple—we'll turn 'em all off manually.*

Forty minutes later, climbing into bed, we realized we'd turned off our bedside lamps and couldn't get them back on— which would be no obstacle for some, but I haven't gone to sleep without reading first since before I could read. However, I soldiered on and eventually fell asleep counting my blessings, only to wake up after a few minutes with the distinct feeling of being watched.

I looked up and noticed a can light we'd been unable to douse, which was illuminating a very big, very alive-looking wild boar trophy—his beady black eyes, large snout, and menacing tusks giving this fairly intrepid *Flower* girl a bit of a fright. After waking my husband to switch places with me, he harrumphed, "Great, now we're both awake."

The next day was as wonderful as the one before, filled with gorgeous people, places, and parties, but we were met with the same technical difficulties come bedtime. Though we progressed to figuring out how to leave our bedside lamps on for reading, the can light still defiantly shone—all night—on the wild boar.

After our third day, which was a replica of the first two only even more wonderful, as I lay in our cocoon-like bed gazing up at the boar, still brilliantly illuminated by the recalcitrant can light, something in me took over. I was seized with a burning desire and determination to TURN THAT LIGHT OFF.

I crept around, found the keypad, and began to punch every square on the board. Of course, all the lights came on, went off, some stayed on, some extinguished—flood lights, kitchen lights, bedroom chandelier light, porch lights, mudroom lanterns, on and on.

Then suddenly, on the verge of giving up, I found myself in total darkness—total—even the boar was in darkness. I squealed inwardly and jumped back into bed. I lay there for a good long while, reveling in my triumph, eager to show off my newfound "techno skills" for my husband the next night, when I suddenly remembered with sad irony, *Dang it, we're leaving tomorrow.* ⚜

Rose Bush sees
red taillights in

braving atlanta

"SO ROSE, WHY ARE YOU GOING TO ATLANTA BY YOURSELF?"
asked one of my best buddies, hand on hip. "Because my
husband [Pastor/MacGyver] cannot accompany me, and I must
go to this fancy-dress ball at the botanical garden. The theme is
floral—floral invitations, floral ball gowns—beyond floral. I gotta

see this! I told him I'd be back Saturday night in time to hear him preach Sunday morning."

I decided to stay at the home of an Atlanta *Flower* girl the night before the ball. Since she was traveling that weekend, I agreed to take care of the livestock—one dear rescue dog named Roxie.

On the day of the ball I visited some advertisers and worked on the classes for a flower show I'd been put in charge of. Although I was in unfamiliar surroundings, all went smoothly. I packed up my car and arrived at the ball right on time (early to meet with the photographer). I roamed around the venue admiring the sunset colors of the evening's décor, met the caterer, and took scouting shots with my phone.

As the party began to pick up, I cast about to meet the floral designers and find my table. Ha! I found them. I was seated at their table—love when that happens.

The evening was superb—delightful dinner partners to my left and right, tinkling of glasses and swishing of ball gowns, swell strains of some of my favorite standards, and lovely tributes to those who helped the Garden grow. But like Cinderella, I had to leave before the end of the ball—in my case, so that my hybrid Tahoe (or as I lovingly call it, "the Hy-hoe") didn't turn into a pumpkin. I really wanted to get home to Birmingham in time to get a good night's sleep.

Discreetly slipping out, I looked back and savored the rosy glow of the tent filled with flowery dresses and the black and white of tuxedos. As I strolled across the brow of the gardens, gradually the big band sounds were replaced by the driving beat of Coldplay, in concert just below at Piedmont Park. What a sublime moment—worlds colliding, or rather overlapping. I felt suspended in time and wonder as I strolled out to the valet parker.

"Hope you had a lovely evening. Do you need directions, ma'am?" asked the valet.

"No, thank you. I've got it. This rig has an awesome GPS. It practically drives itself," I tossed back to him.

And then I was off. I knew to head to I-75 and then to I-20, and I'd be on my way. With the help of my GPS I got right to I-75, no sweat. And then I sat in bumper-to-bumper traffic for what seemed like an hour... as far as the eye could see, red taillights—not-moving, red taillights.

I finally exited, thinking I'd take an alternate route to I-20. I headed over the interstate on the exit ramp, and looking westward to I-20... again, a sea of red taillights—not-moving, red taillights.

Frustrated, I called MacGyver and described the situation. His response was, "Well, honey, can you just find a hotel downtown and spend the night and get up early?"

Music to my ears. *Hello, Four Seasons?*

Approaching the reception desk, I realized I had left my big purse at our *Flower* girl's home way up north of town. Yikes.

Luckily, I know my American Express number by heart and had stayed at this particular hostelry in the past, so they put me up for the night.

I set my alarm for dawn-thirty and blearily set off to retrieve my purse. On arrival, I saw that Roxie's dish was empty, and since her parents weren't due in till that night, I filled it with food, topped off her water, then went in and grabbed my handbag.

On returning to the car, I realized there were no keys to be found. Thus far, I had been fairly Zen about all the twists and turns, but at this point, I lost it. I started shrieking and yanking everything out of the car and looking under bushes. I even moved Roxie's bowl. Nothing. Nowhere. No keys.

Dejected, I sat on the stoop, watched Roxie eat, and had a good cry. I finally reached in my pocket to call MacGyver and warn him that I would most likely miss church, and... pulled out my car keys.

As I pulled out of the driveway, while Roxie's head was buried in her bowl, blissfully unaware of my trials and tribulations, a familiar voice crooned from the radio: Chris Martin, of Coldplay, singing, "Everything's Not Lost."

Yeah, if I hadn't gotten all Shanghai'd and turned around, Roxie might have missed breakfast. ⚜

Rose Bush gets rained on in

weather or not

ONE OF MY TOP 10 WEDDING DON'TS IS: If you don't want to sweat the weather, don't have your wedding outside. So one would think I would mind my own list of don'ts, but recently, I didn't. I was planning an office party/surprise unveiling of our new *Not So Prim Rose* book at the *Flower* International Headquarters (the "IHQ," as we call it), a quaint shake cottage with an ample backyard. And since the mean age of the *Flower* girls (other than me) is 25, I thought, *Hey, wouldn't it be cool to get a food truck to pull up and serve outside! We've never done that before, and these* *girls would LOVE it.* Plus, I knew it would be casual and less work for me—easy breezy.

Breezy is right. And rainy. And cold. So much for my hip idea. But the youngsters running the food truck were plucky and game and spent the entire night running with umbrellas and gourmet grilled cheese sandwiches and yummy, creamy tomato soup, followed by plated desserts into the IHQ. I, on the other hand, spent the entire night running behind folks, mopping up rainwater, praying no one would slip if I missed a spot, and apologizing for the weather ('cause that's something I'm in charge of).

The party ended with all the guests relatively unscathed, if a tad soggy, and me semi-bedraggled but grateful for the minimal amount of drama. "Phew!" I exclaimed. "Another one in the books."... as I dodged puddles and mud on the way to my car parked in the backyard.

Settling in and looking forward to a hot shower and warm bed, I eased the car into reverse and promptly went nowhere. Yep, my car was stuck in the mud. Too tired to scream, I did the next best thing: I called my husband (whom many of you know as MacGyver) and asked him to come get me. Pulling into the backyard in our 1989 Jeep Wagoneer, he hopped out with a tow rope and all the other necessary paraphernalia to extract my car from the mud.

At which point, I laughed, grabbed him by the collar, and dragged him back to the Jeep to ferry me home. Another one in the books all right—the next *Not So Prim Rose* book. ⸸

Rose Bush testifies
that beauty
is in fact pain in
spa mistreatment

THOSE WHO KNOW ME WELL can testify to my "tomboy-ness" and my lack of enthusiasm re: all things cosmetic. However, as much as I travel and speak to large groups of women in the name of *Flower*, it has become a necessary evil for me to pay homage to Aphrodite. Evil is the operative word. Allow me to recount my most recent brush with the puckish deity. It all started when I took a day off on the heels of a jam-packed three weeks of travel and deadlines.

I thought to myself, *It's been a while since I submitted to the monster that is the microdermabrasion machine. Let's do it!* While at the spa, I decided to load up on treatments so I wouldn't have to come back for a while. Note to self: Microdermabrasion followed by face waxing equals pain, inflammation, and some red spots that are still apparent a week later. But I cheered up, knowing I had a shellac manicure and massage still to come.

The shellac manicure, though not a walk in the park (what with the stripping of the old polish in a somewhat ungentle manner), is not usually unbearable, except when it is—like on this particular spa visit. For some reason the manicurist thought that orange wood sticks were not pointed and would not hurt when she dug them into the tops of my nails with all her might.

Three yelps later she finally got the message and lightened up. (I could see traces of bruising under the nail—good thing I was getting dark polish.)

My last hope for a positive spa experience was my massage. After scanning the mile-long menu, I closed the brochure and said, "I'll just have a plain ol' Swedish, light pressure." The masseuse looked crestfallen and began with resignation. "Now if the pressure's too hard, you just let me know," she instructed.

She then proceeded to massage my limbs and back with what can only be described as a vengeance. I let her know several times that the pressure was too hard, and she would relent for a minute and then lapse right back into a pounding, almost brutal pressure.

Finally, I sat up and looked her in the eye (through the haze of tiger balm and Eastern elevator music) and said, "YOU ARE HURTING ME!" She looked contrite and dejected and proceeded to finish the hour with a half-hearted effort, and I fairly sprung up when she finished. Usually masseuses ask, "How do you feel?" at the end of a treatment. She knew better.

I must have looked pretty rough when I arrived home from my "day of beauty," as my mother used to call it, because my husband took one look at me and said, "Honey, you look like you've had a rough day. Here, lemme rub your back."

Rose Bush
locks herself in
the loo in
stuck & amok

"WE ARE SO EXCITED to get to shoot your gardens, y'all. Thank you! I just *LOVE* how you've made this Connecticut field look like a hillside in Provence! Oh I know it's early, and I'm so sorry— no, please do go get dressed! We're just gonna scout around. And 'course I'd love to talk to y'all about all your plantings and your vision and all. We're comin' back tomorrow for the official house and garden tour too! Can't wait!! You just lemmeno when you're ready. We'll be right here."

As my barrage of folksy Southern-ness trailed off, the shell-shocked homeowners turned and retreated into the house. These two cosmopolitan professionals had agreed to let us photograph the gardens of their country house before a garden tour the next day, but were woefully unprepared for the likes of me. (In case you haven't guessed, I'm a morning person.)

The morning consisted of me and the photographer traipsing around with the garden designer of the pair, and me grilling him about EVERYTHING in sight. When we left I thought I heard a slight sigh of relief (or maybe it was the wind).

Fast-forward to the next afternoon. I had saved this house and garden for last on the tour, as I wanted to really linger in the gardens and spend time touring the interior. I made my way around the gardens and all the tourers and then repaired to the inside. *What a stunning world these two inhabit!*

Meandering into the last bedroom, I took the liberty of using the W.C. before getting in the car to head back to NYC. Of course, like the rest of the house, it was beautiful—with a blue-and-white Peter Dunham print on the shower and window and even an old copy of *Vanity Fair* whose cover was all blues and whites—such a crisp and polished loo! I had plenty of time to observe these details, because, as I attempted to exit, the door decided not to cooperate.

I tried and tried, held my mouth right, even said a prayer, but it wouldn't budge. Now, I was already on a bit o' thin ice with these lovely weekenders, what with our predawn arrival the day before and my bull-in-a-china-shop, boy-howdy ways. And now, I was going to be their uninvited houseguest.

After a stretch of sitting and reading the old *Vanity Fair*, I hatched a plan: I waited till other tourers entered the room, and then I screamed for help. None of them could affect even the slightest progress in the stuck-door scenario, so someone went of to get one of the homeowners. *Cringe.*

The genteel, sophisticated owner, who also happened to be the architect of the house, came to my rescue with a calm, "Just push on the bottom of the door, and I'll pull." And presto! As the door flew open, I was welcomed by the crowd that had gathered and, ham that I am, bellowed, "Free at Last!!!" etc... which I imagine is what the couple muttered as I drove off for the last time. ⚡

Rose Bush
airs her dirty
laundry in

hard pressed

THOUGH NOT A CLOTHESHORSE PER SE, I do like to appear clean
and fresh whenever I travel to represent *Flower*. Thanks to lots
of wash-and-wear and travel irons in hotels, I'm able to achieve
this, for the most part—unless the airline throws a wrench in the
works, as on a recent trip to a garden symposium in Louisiana.
There was only one plane change, but my little red bag wanted to
stay in Atlanta—and I did not.

Met by two gregarious, gardeny men at the airport, I was then assured by the airline representative that my bag would be delivered, posthaste, to the small, charming town where I was presenting.

For some reason I had decided to travel in a dressier-than-usual floral top and nice cotton pants (almost like I knew). Though this outfit served me well and was pretty appropriate for the first night's casual supper, I was hoping to have my bag waiting for me when I returned to my hotel later that night. Nope.

The sweet, gardeny men felt sorry for me and ran me by the dollar store—a first for me. We were on a mission to find a nightgown and some toiletries. (I have not seen Prell shampoo since I went to camp as an adolescent.) Racing through the aisles, giggling like children, looking for sundries, we ended up at a rack of nightgowns. After spinning the rack a time or two, we all settled on a lovely leopard/floral–print mumu that had my name written all over it!

Fast-forward to my presentation the next day: I shared with a friend at the venue my tale of wardrobe deficit, to which she responded, "Oh, you look great! Just don't say anything. No one would ever guess." To which I retorted, "Are you kidding?? This is the stuff people love to hear about. Plus, it's going in my next Not So Prim Rose column."

Back to my hotel and—still no bag. So I pressed my floral blouse and nice cotton britches for the third time. I was starting to feel really confident in my ironing skills (an unforeseen silver lining).

That evening I arrived at a party with all the same people,

sporting my now-familiar and much-remarked-on outfit. Which was fun and funny, but at the same time, everyone else at this point was dressed to the nines for the final soirée, and my clothes were looking a little tired and smelling a little gamey.

At the end of the evening, en route back to the hotel in a car full of speakers and symposium bigwigs, I got a call from a nice man named Tobey who had my bag and was lost and, "Could we please just rendezvous at the Exxon station in downtown St. Petersville?" *Of course!* I was *SO* relieved to have my bag, just in time to have a fresh ensemble for my crack-of-dawn trip home the next day.

Settling back into my room and trying to maintain my what-the-heck attitude, I turned to unzip my little red bag to get out my un-leopardish nightgown and could not help but burst out laughing with a "Yeah, right!" as I looked down and noticed a discreet, little apologetic tag on my bag that said: *Sorry for the delay. –Alpha Airlines*

Rose Bush
dresses to impress in

shut the front dior

"ROSE, YOU JUST GOT AN INVITATION to Martha Stewart's American Made Awards! You've got to go!" cheered my assistant.
OMGoodness! What shall I wear?!? Well it's NYC, so black of course—no brainer. I have a cute little black dress, and I can buff up these old Fendi patent pumps and should be good to go. OK, if I

was going to fly up to the Big Apple for a "fahncy" party, I had to make it make sense financially.

So, I scheduled meetings with advertisers and newsstand folks trying to do some business while in town, booked the least-expensive hotel room without bedbugs I could find, did NOT have a facial, did my own hair, and even committed to forego room service (which ended up being a hollow sacrifice, as my bedbug-free economy hotel didn't offer it).

On my way back to my hotel after a day of meetings, I happened to find myself on Fifth Avenue, and happened to veer into Saks. I immediately began to doubt my understated sartorial selections. *This is Martha Stewart for cryin' out loud! This is NYC! This is fancy! I need to step it up! But I don't have time to try on a million dresses... Oh I know—a statement bag!*

So, thinking that I'd just get a small clutch that had a logo buckle or something, not spend a lot, just get something chic and recognizably swell, I lasered over to the purses. Nothing caught my eye till I recognized this little black patent-leather quilted number with two handles and a big silver Dior zipper chain. Not being a Dior aficionado, I assumed it was pricey but not outrageously so. I picked it up, held it in the mirror, and I was sold.

I whipped out my plastic, all the while chatting with a lovely fellow shopper and the oh-so-sleek salesman, and proceeded to sign the receipt. The effort I made at not choking when I saw the price was priceless, and I managed to stifle an expletive in the bargain. Of course, backing out was out of the question—I was in way too deep at this point.

So I scurried out of the store with my new "statement bag" in a bag, and hightailed it to the hotel to do my own hair, don my LBD and almost-vintage pumps, thinking, *Well, I've spent a lot of money, but it's worth it. I feel armed and ready. Sophisticated, celebrity-filled New York gig here I come!*

I arrived at the venue to a sea of black cocktail clothes. Of course. Though a brilliant evening full of incredibly talented folks and presentations, the event was so well attended, I found myself shoulder to shoulder in a throng of attendees all night long. So, short of holding the bag on my shoulder like a boom box or up in the air like a protest sign, there was no way for anyone to be impressed with my new statement bag.

Striding back to my hotel, I resolved to carry this new bag every chance I got so that, though it would not pay for itself, I would get my money's worth. My husband began to question my taste (and sanity) when I carried it on the skiff when we went bone fishing, but I was determined.

I even considered sharing this silly tale with Ms. Stewart when I interviewed her for a story in this issue, but thought, *Naahh, I'd rather talk flowers. Plus, who knows, she may even read this.*

Rose Bush causes a rural ruckus in

lost & found

FOR ALMOST A MONTH, my husband and I have been going back and forth about whether to take the seats out of our Hy-hoe (my nickname for our hybrid Tahoe) in order to transport a ton of hydrangea and some bundles of elaeagnus from a North Alabama grower to our assistant editor's

{ NOT SO PRIM ROSE }

wedding that I was "helping" with in South Alabama.

I was for—he was against. He won and folded the seats down, loaded me up, and off I went to Tiny Town, Alabama. When I arrived at the wedding site—Cherokee Ridge, the bride's family farm/compound—I immediately asked if I might stash my new striped purse in the house out of the heat.

Then, after conferring about a few logistics, storing three huge bunches of elaeagnus in the cool of the family chapel, and watching the landscaper peel slices of Irish Spring into the caladium to keep the deer away (I thought, *Heck that would keep me away*.), I went on a golf cart tour of the compound, insisting all the while that I didn't want to be any trouble, and I knew there wasn't time for this, and I really needed to get out of their way. When we arrived back at the cars, I thanked my tour guide, hopped into the Hy-hoe, and roared off to check in to my motel.

Making a quick stop at a Piggly Wiggly to pick up some healthy food items, I suddenly realized I had left my purse 30 minutes away at the Ridge. After I finished my self-flagellation, I remembered MacGyver had handed me some cash on my way out the door, so I was able to eat that night. But then, how would I pay for my motel?

Luckily, I was in Tiny Town, Alabama, and luckily, I am such a veteran online shopper that I know my Amex number by heart, so I was able to not only eat, but sleep that night. I did, however, text and call the bride ('cause she didn't have anything else going on) to alert her to my emergency purse situation—but realized there was no cell service out on the Ridge and her parents' landline was conveniently out of order. Oh well, I knew I'd be out there the next day.

Along with transporting plant material, I had been enlisted to help the local florist implement the bride's vision for her wedding. When I walked into the shop the next morning, I sized up the situation pretty dang quick. These small-town flower ladies were big-city talented, but the work space was the size of a walk-in closet, so my main job was going to be to stay out of the way.

I tried my rusty hand at a couple of smaller arrangements, prepped a few buckets of flowers, and then graciously offered to make deliveries to the wedding venue. I knew where it was, and oh yeah, I could retrieve my purse.

Though I really didn't want to disrupt the family's prewedding visiting and chores, 20 minutes after I delivered the flowers, the bride, her mother, aunt, two cousins, the wedding coordinator, and three young nephews were all on the hunt for my bag, to no avail. I finally gamely shrugged and thanked them all, assuring them I could do without my credit cards until MacGyver arrived, and I started back into town.

While backing up the car, I noticed a blur of white and gray underneath the folded-down seat. Yep, it was my purse.

For a minute I considered not telling, I was so chagrined, but I didn't want the case of the missing purse to hang over the festivities, so I jumped out and sheepishly confessed to the bride who, in true *Flower* girl form, immediately chirped, "Maybe this can be a Rose story!" ❧

Rose Bush suffers
the stings and harrows of
outrageous fortune in

pest control

UNLIKE MOST REPORTS FROM THE ROAD, this one contains a few unrelated minor mishaps—more like a series of *SNL* sketches than a half-hour sitcom. It all started when I traveled to New York for two photo shoots and about 10 or 12 meetings, sans assistant—my first mistake. I had eschewed the extra expense, confident of my ability to handle labyrinthine logistics with ease and aplomb.

The meetings were standard operating procedure, so not too much trouble there, until I had a breakfast meeting with one of my floral and event design heroes I'd been desperate to meet.

We met at a chic downtown hotel and chatted over omelets. Things were going swimmingly, till I, wildly gesticulating with my fork, dropped a mushroom down my bra. At first I tried to ignore it and continue our bubbly repartee, but soon found I could not concentrate. I took the bull by the horns and stated matter of factly, "I'm sorry, but I have a mushroom down my bra. Do you mind if I retrieve it?" To which he burst out laughing and entreated me to do so.

Soooo, needless to say, all ice broken—and any illusions of my being an elegant, poised, sophisticated lady—dashed. (Why I didn't simply excuse myself and beat it to the powder room, I will never know.)

My next hiccup happened while schlepping donated Dutch flowers from the flower district to the rental car agency at LaGuardia to the hotel on Long Island for a photo shoot the next day. I had borrowed buckets in the flower district, and purchased a few at the Home Depot behind the hotel, and set about prepping the flowers when I realized I still had many bunches of blooms out of water. So I did what any resourceful *Flower* girl would do—I filled up both wastebaskets and the ice bucket with water and finished cleaning the flowers.

All was well until I had to transport the flowers to the photo shoot and got into a bit of a tussle with the manager on duty at the hotel. I asked to take the wastebaskets full of flowers but promised to return them, offered to leave my designer handbag as collateral, and even threw in the offer of a free year's subscription to *Flower*—nothin' doin'. He pointed to the door and bid me a curt adios.

Then, driving for 35 minutes with the A.C. cranked to subarctic temperatures to keep the flowers happy, I arrived on location— trembling, teeth chattering, and my still-wet hair somewhat frozen, which actually came in handy, as the shoot was outside on the hottest day of the summer.

And speaking of heat, you know who loves heat? Wasps. So, I was walking around barefooted trying to be all cool and comfy in the garden when I felt a sharp stab in my right big toe. Apparently I was treading on Mr. Wasp's turf. *Uggghhhh.*

Nothing to do, but soldier on. All the flowers, food, china, silver, and linens were set up, and I was hobbling around getting in the stylist's way when suddenly a swarm of flies attacked the food. *What????*

Oh yeah, that's right, we'd set up the shoot about 30 yards from the polo pony barn. We tried fly spray, swatting, even yelling "Shoo!" at the top of our lungs, to no avail. Every time we'd shoo them away, they would come back brazenly. So it was this crazy dance of me, the photographer's assistant, and the stylist shooing, jumping out of the frame, the photographer shooting, and us starting the whole routine again.

While on the phone recounting the day to my husband and complaining about my level of exhaustion, I searched bravely for a silver lining and realized I could get out of the forced march at my oh-so-fit cousin's beach house the next day. ⚘

Rose Bush braves air travel and computer mayhem, and lives to write about it in

tech no!

I CONSIDER MYSELF A SEASONED AND SAVVY TRAVELER, for the most part, and a pretty darned good sport in the face of most setbacks. I'm even aware that with each delay, the odds that a flight will ultimately get canceled increase exponentially. However, like all optimists, I think to myself, *It won't happen to ME, not AGAIN*. But, en route from New York to Jacksonville,

Florida, for an antiques show, my equanimity was truly tested.

After a whirlwind 36 hours in the Big Apple scouting, selling, and socializing, I screeched up on two wheels to the airline curbside check-in, barely making the required arrival one-hour ahead of flight time. I raced to security, only to be met by, of course, a line that defied the laws of physics.

Miraculously, I made it to my gate before the scheduled departure time, and promptly encountered a delay—not just a slight delay, but a four-hour delay. At which point I decided to trade the Coney Island-ness of the under-construction concourse for the Alpha Cloud Club (a seasoned, savvy traveler move). I proceeded to find my bivouac, which included an outlet for technology and a table for my iPad near the snack island, but secluded enough to concentrate on writing my intro for the world-famous designer I was to introduce in Jacksonville.

I was just settling in when I got a call from Paces Blue, the other world-famous interior designer scheduled to speak in Jacksonville the next morning. He was at the gate, and wanted to compare notes. I bid him come to the Cloud Club. After some requisite grousing and checking on the delay status, we settled into our respective spots and each got to work.

After a while I'd come up with what I thought was the perfect intro for the illustrious designer—just the right mix of praise, humor, and concision—and emailed it to one of our editors to proof. I heard it swoosh, so I knew it went. She never got it, nor was it in my sent folder. I HATE technology.

I decided to check on the flight again and immediately

regretted it, as it had been delayed another three hours. I, as a sponsor and introducer, was expendable. Paces Blue, as the first presenter the next morning, was not. We talked to the ladies in Jacksonville numerous times, trying to anticipate every eventuality, including flight cancellation, which would mean he would be unable to make the 10 a.m. gig the next day.

Then, as we were sitting back down, we heard the dreaded announcement—our flight had been canceled. Deleted expletive!!

Paces called the ladies, and I tried to reach cousins on the West Side for a bed, to no avail. So Paces gallantly offered his sofa, but I insisted that after nine hours in the Cloud Club we could both do with a little privacy. And besides, the airline was offering vouchers for a hotel. Or not. By the time I got up to the desk, they were all gone. I called a few hotels in the city, bit the bullet, and taxied back the way I came.

By then, the streets looked like the city was in the middle of a garbage strike, a steady rain was falling, and the bodega where I stopped to buy a toothbrush and toothpaste (I had opted to leave my luggage where it was—checked) only took cash. Who has cash?! Not me.

So, the next morning, fortifed by a few hours of sleep and packing a really bad case of panther breath, I returned to my home away from home, waltzed through security—no wait, onto the plane—and sat smack-dab across from the world-famous interior designer I was to introduce. Maybe she could help me with my rewrite. She certainly knew the subject.

On arrival, we got in the car with the gracious lady in charge of meeting us at the airport and began to chat about the event. She immediately described Paces' presentation in glowing terms. *WHAAAATT?*

Had he chartered a private plane? Ridden a speeding train through the night? Been teleported? Nope. The brilliant ladies had Skyped him in to the breathlessly anticipating crowd, who proceeded to give him a standing ovation. I LOVE technology! ⚡

Rose Bush realizes
everyone needs an editor in

rsvp-o'd!

AS HAS BEEN EVINCED ON EARLIER OCCASIONS, I have an opinion or two, and some might even say I'm intransigent. I like a handwritten thank-you note, hometown weddings, "you're welcome" rather than the oft-used and utterly meaningless "no problem," and paper (not electronic) invitations for parties, preferably letterpress and defnitely hand-addressed. (If you're too busy to write them, you're too busy to have a party.)

So what fun when I heard my godchild and namesake was getting married and I was going to host the brunch! Since she lives far away, one of the cohosts from her hometown handled all local logistics. Perfect. "I'll handle the invitations," I volunteered, mentally rubbing my hands together glecfully, and thinking to myself, *If anyone has a problem with the expense of the letterpress, I'll eat the overage.* (They didn't.)

One call and two emails later, the invitations were settled on. The couple lives in the Florida Keys and loves to fish and sail, so I selected a jaunty, stylized knotted rope for the motif (wondering if anyone would catch the "tying the knot" visual pun) and a playful but still elegant font. Before pulling the trigger, I checked the spelling of all words and names repeatedly, even my own phone number, as it wouldn't do for some unsuspecting resident to receive boatloads of RSVPs on his or her voice mail, all the while me marveling at the rudeness of the entire guest list.

Finally satisfed, I gave the all systems go and patted myself on the back for the chic cleverness of my creation. A few weeks later, I found myself at my dining room table addressing, stuffing, sealing (licking), and stamping the 175 invitations. Once mailed,

I rested in the glow of self-satisfaction at a job beautifully done, and the pleasure I would have receiving compliments from all quarters once RSVPs started pouring in.

As you may have guessed, that is not at all how things unfolded. My first voice mail response was a "Hi, Rose! I can't wait to come to the brunch," quickly followed breezily with, "By the way, I'm sure you didn't mean to put AUGUST 27th instead of APRIL 27th. Just wanted you to know."

All blood drained from my face as I muttered a phrase that can't be repeated (at least not in print). When I recovered a modicum of composure, I took a look at the invitation proof, aaaaannnnd... Yes, I had approved August rather than the correct April.

So without hesitation, I ordered "oops" correction cards, hand-addressed them, and sent them out ASAP. I really didn't have time, this time, but I made time. I couldn't stand to think of one person showing up at the house in August, only to fnd the host family away for the summer. Besides, I would hate for anyone to think I hadn't caught my mistake (which I hadn't—thank goodness for the first responder!).

The day of the brunch dawned with my hoping all had received the second round. But after all the consternation, I can't tell you the number of guests who mentioned how surprised they were to get the "oops" card, as they hadn't even noticed the wrong date.

I did not, however, receive any compliments on the actual invitation, which I believe was overshadowed by the "oops." From now on, I vow to run all copy by the crackerjack editorial team at the magazine. ⚜

Rose Bush takes to the highway and encounters a few potholes in

ire and rain

"HONEY, DON'T LEAVE YOUR SUITCASE OPEN. You know what always happens!" If only I'd listened to those loving and sage words from my husband, MacGyver. But, after all, I was only running downstairs to grab some items from the laundry room. Surely my cat, Minuit, wouldn't have time to show her displeasure with my impending departure for Kentucky in her usual charming urinary way.

Two phone calls and 15 minutes later, I too late realized the error of my ways when, on returning to my room, I smelled the all-too-familiar odor of my cat's disapproval. It's never a good thing to have cat urine on your clothes and in your valise, but, as you might imagine, when traveling for *Flower* I tend to pack my best and favorite fashions.

So, throwing the entire case into the tub, and grabbing the handheld shower nozzle, I did what any hurried, harried, non-domestic goddess would do: I hosed the whole mess down. Again, I too late realized several of my favorite items were silk— not to mention the fact that I didn't have time to wash and dry anything anyway. Hello quick trip to Saks en route out of town. *Cha-ching, cha-ching, cha-ching.* Sweet MacGyver didn't even say, "I told you so," as I ran back to the car with an armload of new traveling clothes.

Things were looking up until he received a call from a neighbor that they had seen Finnegan, our daughter's Irish wolfhound/ small horse (who was staying at our house with the house sitter) down on the main road trotting toward the highway. (He was not going to be left behind, especially with that ornery Minuit.) Sooooo, another 15 minutes added on to our time as we circled back and wrestled Finnegan into the back of my not-very-large and now-filled-with-new-clothes-and-luggage car. The livestock seemed to be against us.

Finally on the road to Kentucky, we breathed a sigh of relief and began to look forward to a few days in the Bluegrass with some of our favorite *Flower* friends. It was going to be smooth sailing from there on—until we stopped halfway to gas up. MacGyver, usually a master of all things car-and-truck related filled my non-diesel-powered car with—yep, you guessed it— diesel fuel. Forty-five minutes later, having borrowed a siphon from an obliging truck driver, and gotten all of the offending fuel out, we proceeded to gas up, again, and hit the road. (And yes, we had to pay for both tankfuls.)

Many of you at this point might have turned back, thinking the trip ill-fated. Not us. We turned our faces like flint to the north, listened to some mood-elevating Motown, and pressed on. When we finally arrived and the skies opened up between our car and our cottage, drenching us in that way that only a summer downpour can do, I simply threw my head back and laughed. I was, after all, wearing all cotton. ❦

{ NOT SO PRIM ROSE }

ONE OF THE THINGS I TAKE FOR GRANTED and sometimes pride myself in is my natural athletic ability. I've never aspired to greatness but have always enjoyed being quick to pick up a sport, and be fairly proficient. Chief among these sports is tennis. Though I no longer play team tennis (4.0-4.5, a solid 'B' player) or compete in tournaments, I still enjoy playing singles with my husband (a more recent convert to the game) from time to time. And by enjoy, I mean relish. And by playing, I mean thrashing him every time. Though not speedy or particularly strong, I've always been able to "put it where he ain't." Our habit in the last few years has been to tune in to the four Grand Slam tournaments (Wimbledon and the Australian, French, and US Opens), watch until our vision blurs, then jump up from the sofa, don our whites, and proclaim with gusto, "We can do that!"

This summer, he started taking lessons. I did not. Why should I? I'm a natural, I've been playing my whole life, I was a club kid, I've got this.

It was soon after Wimbledon that I realized our rallies were becoming longer, his serve was getting stronger, and, though I was still emerging victorious, I was actually having to work for it. *Hmmm.*

Most recently, true to our MO and inspired by the US Open, we got fired up and, though it was excruciatingly hot and humid, stormed the courts. And then, something really strange happened—he beat me. Not only did I NOT put it where he wasn't, I kept hitting it right to him, or he got to every shot. I did not. He served aces several times. I double-faulted into the double digits, hurled numerous expletives, and—the crowning blow—while backpedaling for an overhead, tripped over myself and oh-so-gracefully fell flat on my derrière. I tried desperately to feign injury and put myself out of misery, but I couldn't pull it off.

Actually, the real crowning blow was his innocently remarking on the redness of my face, and asking if I wanted to quit. Nope.

I played my best till the bitter end, and then, head hung in defeat, texted the pro for his first available lesson. By the Australian Open in January, I plan to reclaim my title. ✢

Rose Bush gets "picked" in

pinky swear

"DOGS AND CATS LIVING TOGETHER, MASS HYSTERIA." –Bill Murray's take on the situation in *Ghostbusters* is a refrain that continues to float across my psyche.

Ours is a house where cats and dogs live separately, i.e. two male bird dogs in the mudroom and outside, and two house cats who rule with iron paws. Generally, never the twain meet, but on one chaotic December morning, when racing out to work my garden club greenery sale, I left the mudroom door into the kitchen open and all *H* broke loose. Dashin' Conrad, our Llewellin Setter, lunged into the house and went straight for my darling black cat, Minuit.

I, in turn, lunged for his collar and proceeded to see my pinky finger bend at an angle I've never seen before and hope to never see again. Minuit was howling, Dash was growling, and I was cussing. It was mass hysteria. I finally wrestled him out the door, stuck my hand in the icemaker, and cried for a bit. But, the greenery sale was waiting, and so off I went.

One of my favorite things about the sale is the camaraderie in the back room while we put together Christmas arrangements.

Every year, I'm right in the middle of two of my favorite women in town, who also happen to be two of the funniest. They're my mother's generation and possess that priceless mix of Southern charm and elegance peppered with major irreverent sass.

So, when I walked in, holding my pinky—now swollen, and black and blue—they showed the requisite concern, and then proceeded to craft a splint consisting of two green flower picks (with the points cut off) wrapped around my digit with green floral tape, all the while tossing off one-liners and puns. This morphed into a major moment, with other members gathering around, summoning the historian to photograph the two triage nurses wrapping my faux splint for the garden club scrapbook.

I told the duo I was due at the orthopedic doctor later that day on an unrelated matter, and they began to swell with pride and made me promise to show him their handiwork, which I did.

Thinking he would scoff, rip it off, and replace it with a for-real splint, I was pleasantly surprised and proud of my first responders when he examined it and said, with a wry smile, "I couldn't have done better myself."

Rose Bush
tries—and fails—to
rock the boat in

smooth

sailing

ALL MY PREVIOUS DISPATCHES from life as a *Flower* editor have been tales of air-travel mishaps, party fiascos, destructive pets, wardrobe malfunctions, technical difficulties, car crises, and even non-life-threatening, on-the-job injury. As we approach deadline, the editorial team has begun to hover a bit and periodically ask if I will have a new Not So Prim Rose. I continue to respond, with a shrug of the shoulders, "Not yet—no embarrassing moments at speaking engagements, no debacles, no horror stories. Not one, nada, nothing."

Most people would be thrilled. I, however, have grown fond of mining those blunders and bungles for Rose gold. I miss her. I've gone back through my calendar, journal, even my Instagram account to see if maybe I've missed something, but I find only happy days, successful trips, and relatively tame animals, save the occasional carnage when UPS leaves a package. Even my luggage has taken to arriving when I do, where I do. Basically smooth sailing... Surely this can't go on! Heck, I've even gotten to the point where I might have to borrow someone else's troubles. Things have gotten *that* good.

Meanwhile, I guess I should rejoice in all this calm, as I'm soon to depart for the U.K. where I'm sure to wear the wrong footwear on a garden tour and end up knee-deep in a bog, or at the very least, lead the group down some not-so-prim-rose path. Hope springs eternal. ❧

Rose Bush attends
a chichi garden party
and wrestles with
her head covering in *hard hats*

I LOVE A GARDEN PARTY as much as the next *Flower* girl. I enjoy
rocking a pretty frock, sipping a cool drink while chatting,
and admiring a perennial border or a clever hedge treatment.
However, when I'm directed, albeit gently, by my hostess to don
a hat for the occasion, I panic.

The last successful hat-wearing experience I recall was a navy *Madeline* affair with a grosgrain trailing ribbon in third grade. Though I sported an appropriate, straw, broad-brimmed hat for my own garden wedding, the front brim was so big and sat so low, we're still not sure that it was actually me in the pictures. My next millinery effort involved ordering a wool felt Stetson from Orvis in order to look cool and sporty at Thanksgiving on our farm. The pictures from that day have me resembling the Spy vs. Spy guy with the black hat from the old *Mad* magazine days.

Then, this spring, when the French Open was flooding the airwaves, I searched the Internet high and low and ordered a white Panama hat, hoping to look like the dapper tennis fans at Roland Garros. (I always say, "If you can't play good, at least look good.") What arrived a few days into the Open was a hat that was: A) not white—it was more of a dark, dirty sand color; B) not Panama—it came closer to a derby; and C) so small I offered it to my 9-year-old grandson, thinking surely it would fit him. It didn't.

Undaunted—but still hoping to have a hat-happy experience— when I was packing for an English garden tour, I included what I thought was a very Diana, lady-of-the-manor-house kind of hat, thinking I would fit right in with the local swells. I was, however, immediately crestfallen to be told by one of my fellow travelers that I looked like a California hippie. *Bloody H*!

So, it was with some hesitation and trepidation that I searched for a bonnet for the aforementioned fancy garden party, but suddenly remembered I already owned just the thing. I hand-carried a beautiful, straw, flower-trimmed hat (that I'd never worn and only bought as a souvenir) halfway across the country and was sure it was just right for said gathering.

Everyone looked GREAT in their chic chapeaux—everything from fascinators to a simple Panama on one of the male guests. I, however, spent most of the day adjusting my topper, turning the flowers from front to back, and back again, flipping the brim up, then down, and generally feeling self-conscious and somewhat silly.

When the party was over, I removed my hat, brought it home to 'Bama, and promptly gave it to a hat-loving neighbor. She can officially carry it off. Many can. My hat's off to 'em. ⊰

Rose Bush avoids an international incident while dining abroad in

peace meal

NOW, I LOVE WOMEN, and I love travel, and I even love the combination. However, I've never been accused of being a consummate tour guide, and when 18 other flower lovers and I traveled to the U.K., I was thankful for other gifted troop leaders among the group. Most things went surprisingly smoothly, and a good time was had by all. There was, however, this one night in an Italian restaurant in London, where my Southern charm and diplomatic chops were sorely tested.

We arrived late, in waves of three, four, and five, and, on top of that, did not fill the reserved two tables due to a couple of dropouts and a bit of miscalculation. Well, the headwaiter, already flustered by the gaggle of American women, became downright cranky when we informed him that we'd not need the second table. *We were causing so-much-a-trouble!!*

Luckily, the Negronis were already flowing and no one really noticed but me and a few of my compagnos who were seated within earshot. I spent the first part of the evening chatting with my dinner partners, but at the same time eyeing the other empty table nervously, tossing up a prayer for a drop-in group. Well, lo and behold, they appeared and were immediately seated, as if the restaurant had planned for them to be there all along.

So, problem solved. I was happy that the staff was happy. (Wait, is that codependent?) Anyway, the food was superb, the party festive, and I breathed a sigh of relief—until it came time to pay the bill.

One of the other leader-like women casually requested they divide the check by 14. How do you say, "You crazy American tourists—this will cause so much trouble and take way too much time!!!" in Italian? 'Cause I'm pretty sure that's what the waiter said in his mother tongue. But after 10 or 15 minutes of comparing bills, finishing our espressos, and handing them a deck of credit cards, we were paid up and spilling out onto the street.

Again, unskilled travel guide that I am, I had not planned for transportation back to the hotel. Never mind, the restaurant, in their zeal to be rid of us, had arranged for a few cabs. *Phew*.

As I sailed out the door, the headwaiter bid me *arrivederci* and then, surprisingly, double kissed me. Codependent or not, I smiled and was flooded with a warm feeling of having triumphed against all odds, and, at the same time, perhaps having inadvertently mended microcosmic international relations a bit. Bravo.

Rose Bush tries every
trick in the book in

signing bonus

I LOVE ENTERTAINING AT HOME. However, with every party comes a new set of challenges, and a book signing can be particularly tricky. First of all, you're in effect saying to the author, or in this case, authors, *"Sure, we'll have it at my house and I'll turn out all the swells and they'll buy your books and we'll have a grand time."* And then you do everything in your power to ensure all that happens. In my case, I had a fabulous cohost, which started me off ahead of the game. Decisions were made: menu chosen, florist called, invitations ordered, and the date selected—one that would practically guarantee good weather, as it almost never rains in Alabama in the late fall.

So I'm blowing through my week leading up to the party when a friend informs me of the forecast for an incoming storm, exactly when the party is slated to begin. *Super*.

With that, I get on the horn and call my husband (whom regular readers may know as MacGyver), who says not to sweat it. Rather than park in the field where there's true stuck-in-the-mud potential, he suggests the valet guys can pull around to the big, paved empty lot down the street. Easy, breezy. My next call is to my prayer group. Surely 12 folks asking for a weather change will sway the Big Guy. And in between, I'm weighing the merits of covered golf carts, shuttle vans, and golf umbrella–yielding valet parkers. We decide on the latter. My concern at this point is twofold: Will there be any guests, and if there are, how do we reward those hale and hearty partygoers by keeping them dry?

Pretty much everything went according to plan, and in spite of the torrential and ongoing downpour (I'm going to have to fire that prayer group), an abundance of guests streamed in. The party was in full swing, with both authors charming the crowd, signing books, and posing for Instagram pics, when suddenly a breathless valet appeared with the unwelcome news that several cars were stuck.(Apparently the big, paved empty lot was partially sodded—a fact that had escaped my notice for some 20-odd years.)

Again, I turned to MacGyver. Having anticipated just this eventuality, he had purchased a brand-new tow chain and promptly set about the extraction. Sweet, young valet guys, they had never seen the likes of my handy husband. Trying to help, but to not much avail, they finally stood back and let the professional handle it. The next time I saw MacGyver, he was standing by the food table, in a mud- and rain-soaked shirt, mat of gray hair plastered to his head, regaling a gaggle of women with tales of the rescue.

Later, as we bid the last guests farewell and gathered our rain gear to head out to dinner, the deluge suddenly stopped, a gentle breeze blew, and I smiled to myself about the timing. I concluded, with my always-finding-the-pony perspective, that if the weather had been clear, my house could never have held everyone who surely would have appeared. ❧

Rose Bush becomes the toast of the town in

hot pursuit

ONE THING ABOUT ME is that I really do try to promote my friends and *Flower* friends in whatever they're undertaking— sometimes to positive effect, sometimes not so much. And I find in this day of rampant social media and digital wizardry, I have even more opportunities to spread the word via posts, tags, hashtags, etc. But my favorite way to spark sales for people, especially those in the retail fashion world, is the old-fashioned way: Purchase one of their items, sport it, and wait for folks to clamor for sourcing information. "I love that hat! Whose is that?" ...that sort of thing.

So, planning my wardrobe for a recent, big antiques and garden show, and knowing that a major celeb was to be a keynote speaker, I packed strategically, with one particular friend and her warm farm-wear in mind. Since we've had a summer this winter in Birmingham, I was ecstatic that, heading north for the show, I'd no doubt be able to don my super cool, warm and fuzzy cape (hopefully in close proximity to said celeb).

The day of her presentation dawned with the requisite and predicted freezing temperature, and I rejoiced. Carefully choosing the right all-black look to wear under my cape so as not to detract from the actual star of the show (warm and fuzzy cape), and taking way too much time to get my look just right (as if anyone would be looking at me), I raced out into the cold to the venue. Then I sprinted down the football-field length of the conference center—wishing for a Segway—and skidded into the presentation on two wheels.

I thought I was just hot from racing but after a while deduced that the space was, in fact, very warm. No matter, I could open my cape and cool off a bit. Nope, a room with 900 excited people and a heating system that was doing its job sealed my fate. But I was determined. After the presentation I went up and down the line of women, who were waiting for the actress to sign their books, signing them up for *Flower* subscriptions, all the while growing warmer and warmer with the effort—yet still determined not to shed my cape.

Finally, bringing up the rear, book in hand, I asked to have my picture made with the movie star—fingers crossed, hoping and waiting for her to ask about my wrap. Utterly dejected when she didn't, I left, crestfallen. On later glimpsing the photo, I realize I looked as hot (and I don't mean sexy) as I felt: hair showing signs of perspiration, a distinct "glow" on my face, which was decidedly pinker than my blush-on would have produced, and just generally unkempt and uncool.

Running into a good friend on the way out, I was asked, somewhat sheepishly, "Rose, you look like you're burning up. Why don't you take that cape off?" Good question. And the worst part is, so consumed was I with promoting my friend's wares, I forgot to sign the star up for a subscription.

Rose Bush goes where the wild things are in

animal testing

MY HUSBAND AND I ARE ANIMAL LOVERS: he with his 11 bird dogs (nine on the farm and two in town) and me with my three cats (two at home and Marigold at the office). The dogs, or "the boys" as I call 'em, are not the most well-behaved pets in the world, but they're lovable, and can be counted on to bark to blue blazes whenever anyone approaches the house.

Annoyingly, that includes us. They never seem to misbehave when their lord and master is on-site, but rather, choose his absences as opportunities to run amok, and did so again, as recently as yesterday.

'Twas a gray Sunday afternoon, and my husband had gone to the farm. I was looking forward to a post-traveling siesta when the Brittany Spaniel, Louis le Chasseur, limped up to the house, blood running down his leg. I let him in and began my triage. Mid-peroxide pour, in races the other "boy," our Llewellin Setter, Dashin' Conrad Bondhu ("Dash" for short), and all *H* breaks loose! Dash jumps Louis. (I guess it's a bloodlust thing, 'cause they're really good buddies.) Louis fights back, and I commence to scream like unto a banshee, doing all in my power to break it up while still staying out of the fracas. When I see an opening, I grab Louis and hie him to the emergency animal clinic. (Adios, siesta.)

When we arrive, the nurse promptly informs me there are several "patients" ahead of us. I guess weekends are busy in animal emergency rooms, just like in people ones. We sit patiently and watch the colorful, quirky array of people and their pets.

My favorite is the skinny-jeaned, beanie-clad hipster couple who brings in a cage, places it on the counter, and proudly announces that this is their rescue squirrel. They had just adopted him the day before and he was not eating or sleeping. After a while, the couple finishes up checking in their rescue, dubbed Rocky, and repairs to a quiet corner. I am about to return to my reading when the phone rings and I distinctly hear the nurse say, "A sick *alpaca*?!? Well, we're not a large-animal hospital, but our vet does live on a farm. Let me get him."

With those words still hanging in the air, I see a blur of gray/brown speed by and, simultaneously, Louis, miraculously healed, takes off after Rocky across the waiting room floor and into an empty examining room, where the poor, scared squirrel realizes he's got nowhere to run.

The nurse and I nearly collide trying to stop the already traumatized rescue squirrel from being eaten or treed on an exam table. He is able to grab Louis and lead him out while the "parents" scoop up their adoptee. Turns out the door on the cage was not fully locked and they proceed to play the blame game. (Yep, acting like parents already.)

Louis and I are finally settled back down in the waiting room when a big red pickup pulls up and a couple unloads the sick alpaca. I look around for a hidden camera or Ashton Kutcher, but no, this is not an episode of *Punk'd*. I check to be sure my grip on Louis is secure as they bring in their charge. Turns out he had gotten into some azaleas (poisonous to alpacas) and was in need of some animal ipecac.

By this time, Louis' leg injury is seeming pretty pedestrian. But we get it tended to and finally leave the ark. Arriving home, we encounter my just-returning husband who casually asks if I want to take the dogs for a little walk.

My response? Unprintable. *

Rose Bush goes
off the grid in

anti-social media

FOR A SOMEWHAT SENIOR CITIZEN, I'm fairly social-media
savvy, and my favorite platform is Instagram. It's simple and
straightforward. I have found that it is a highly economical way
to view beautiful design, places, and people—especially people.
And I've been known to make a generous donation to attend a

soirée where I'm guaranteed an Insta photo op with the likes of Diane Keaton, or stand in line for hours to be in the frame with Gwyneth Paltrow—like we're best buddies.

My personal Instagram, along with inspiring and amusing me, serves as a pretty reliable chronicle of my activities and encounters. Looking back over a recent trip to NYC, I found lots of shots of places and folks, but there was something missing. I knew something really remarkable had happened, yet I couldn't find it on my feed. (Then it must not have happened—wink emoji.) After replaying my trip visually, I realized there was one location I had neglected to post, and the reason will become clear as you read on.

While NYC is chock-full of shimmery eateries, I gravitate to one in particular for coffee, lunch, or afternoon tea. I find Sant Ambroeus—named after a 4th-century Milanese bishop—with its jaunty green-and-white-stripe awning, delectable fare, and impeccable service, never disappoints.

If I play my cards right, I get a banquette and, looking out, have a wonderful view of some of the city's most interesting and/or glamorous characters. On my most recent visit, however, my lunch partner, unaware of my seating strategy, slid into the banquette, leaving me in a chair with my back to the action. Or so I thought... It was 15-or-so minutes into a lunch brimming with the exhilaration of catching up, when a lithe, elegant, beige-clad figure slipped into the banquette next to us. I glanced over, and then glanced back in shock at my luncheon partner. Our eyes met with that look of, *Yep, that's who you think it is.*

The honey-blond chignon, almond eyes, remarkable cheekbones, perfect amount of jewelry, and effortlessly chic ensemble, all on an impossibly delicate and feminine form, could be none other than Caroline Lee Bouvier Canfield Radziwill Ross, aka Lee Radziwill, aka Jackie's sister. A brief, stunned silence followed— the appropriate moment of digesting that we were sitting within chatting distance of one of the original tastemakers, a Capote swan, a princess. My luncheon partner and I very intentionally continued chatting, trying to act natural, like we were unfazed by this brush with legend. I don't know how we did it.

My greatest challenge, as you can imagine, was to overcome the desire for a pic. My phone sat there, on the table, taunting me. My lunch partner even hatched an elaborate and sneaky plan: I would exit the table for the powder room, phone in hand, and then, as I rounded the corner on my way back, discreetly snap a photo. I nixed the idea, instinctively knowing that this was a moment where discretion would definitely be the better part of valor, and the most discreet and valorous thing I could do would be to leave that legend be. There are some greats whose élan would only be diminished, and never captured, by an appearance on social media, and she is one.

As we left the restaurant, congratulating ourselves on our restraint, I looked down at my phone to check my messages and what to my wondering eyes should appear but a big red bar and the words, "You have 0% charge."

So, as it turns out, I couldn't have "grammed" the princess anyway. I did, however, run back to the hotel to charge up for future sightings. ⬩

Rose Bush
puts it all on in

strip tease

EVERY YEAR IN THE DEAD OF SUMMER, we at *Flower* host a big
shindig in Atlanta where we import a group of design luminaries
from around the land. We host them at a swanky restaurant,
and then the next day, we have a panel discussion followed by
individual presentations, which are always SRO. There are lots

of moving parts, but after five years, it has become pretty much a well-oiled machine. I always want the speakers to be transported in style. This year with everyone staying at the same hotel, I suggested I drive everyone in my husband's (aka MacGyver's) black SUV. The thinking was that we'd look really important, like the President or something, while saving the cost of a limo.

Naturally, wanting the Hy-hoe (as I call MacG's hybrid Tahoe) to look its best, I ran it through the wash the day before driving to Atlanta. As it emerged, I spotted a protrusion I'd forgotten about—the strip of black metal on the front passenger door un-presidentially sticking out almost at a right angle. Well, that wouldn't do for my Very Important Passengers. So lacking the time to visit a body shop and with MacG out of town, I did the next best thing—I consulted my friend Kevin at my neighborhood hardware store. He surveyed the situation and fetched a tube of goop and two wooden two-by-fours. "Just park it next to somethin' hard and flat, glue the strip back, then put one board along the length of it, and "T" it with the other board to hold it in place against somethin' hard and flat—by mornin' it should be stuck good." Sounded simple enough.

When I got home, the only hard and flat thing that I could find to pull the car up to was a hickory tree next to the driveway. I wish you could have seen me trying to park the Hy-hoe the exact distance of the board from the tree. I was hopping in and out, moving the car, wedging the board, getting back in the car to turn it off—the movement of the door jostling the car and making the board drop—with sweat streaming down my face and

"French" words flying the whole time. After the fifth go, the strip stuck. The angels sang.

Even with 70-to-80-mile-an-hour speeds en route to Atlanta, the strip held. I was so proud. I couldn't wait for my husband to see my handiwork. I drove the Talent to dinner, and then to the event the next day, strip intact, and all parts moving smoothly. At the end of the day, driving home to the 'Ham after a triumphant event, I turned my attention to anticipating my husband's glowing praise.

Pulling into the driveway, I called him hoping he had arrived home ahead of me and sneakily asked him to come out and help with my bags. Standing beside the passenger door and beaming with pride, I immediately began crowing about my handyman prowess giving him way too much information about Kevin, goop, the boards, and the like. Then suddenly I heard a *WHOOSH—BOINGGGGG* as the strip popped loose and returned to its earlier angle. More "French," then laughter as MacG lovingly and wryly suggested that I not quit my day job. ⌐

Rose Bush comes to
a stormy conclusion in

hermine made up

I'VE BEEN CALLED MANY THINGS, described many ways—
however, hale and hearty, rough-and-tumble are not among
them. Don't get me wrong; I've overcome plenty of obstacles
in my life, and I can be tough when I need to be. But my go-
to posture at this point in my story is chill, comfortable, and

somewhat pampered. It helps that I'm married to a MacGyver, who indulges me and can do/fix anything. Much as I love finery and luxury, I'm also fond of a bargain. So it was with great glee that I scored what I was sure was a real deal on a seaside cottage rental in the Hamptons over Labor Day. The images online looked quaint and classic in a New England understated way. Right on a little lagoon, it was renting for a song. I couldn't BELIEVE my luck!

However, we arrived after traveling all day and couldn't find the cottage—mainly, because the actual cottage looked NOTHING like the one online. Where it was quaint on the website, it was now dilapidated. Where it was once New England understated, it was now Old England neglected.

But we persevered, sure that the interior would be better. Entering through the back door (there was no front entrance) proved challenging as the knob came off in MacG's hand, and the door itself was stuck to the frame. Eventually, we gained entry but were met with windows with broken panes and ripped screens, floors so slanted I began to fear I was contracting vertigo, and the pièce de résistance—showers that flooded onto the floors. (With the slanting, that meant water running out into the living areas as well as the bathrooms.)

When called, the helpful, affable assistant to the owner assured me that the OUTDOOR shower was new and delightful. Call me old-fashioned (or just call me old), but I prefer to shower indoors with no witnesses from upstairs in the house next door. I'm funny that way.

Luckily, our planned activities took us to beautiful homes, gardens, and venues, and we thoroughly enjoyed the rest of our trip. I was thinking of myself as a pretty good sport and settling into the routine of showering before daybreak (to avoid being seen in my birthday suit by neighbors) when Hurricane Hermine threatened. We thought of leaving but heard reports that the Long Island Expressway was jammed and flights out were completely booked, so we decided to ride out the storm. (I always marvel at those obstinate people who refuse to leave their homes in the face of weather disaster—now I was one of them, and it wasn't even my home.)

As the storm picked up, the homeowner's boat began to toss about, the screen doors began to slam against the side of the house, and the wind blowing through the broken panes began knocking over the myriad tchotchkes belonging to the owner.

Through the night, MacG would go outside and retie the screen doors shut, and we would shift to another bedroom thinking we'd escape some of the wind and rain and noise, but there was nary a quiet, dry spot in the house.

Finally, it was daybreak and we got a reprieve from Hurricane Hermine. My handy husband, after assessing the damage, chirped hopefully that we just needed a little more daylight and a few tools to restore the cottage to a livable level.

He was, however, not completely shocked to find me dressed, packed, and on the phone reserving a room at the nearest posh hotel—which had numerous vacancies due to the storm—for the rest of the trip. A girl can only take so much. ❧

Rose Bush decks
and falls in

o christmas tree, o christmas tree

{ NOT SO PRIM ROSE }

I'M OFTEN HEARD TO PROCLAIM in December, "There are no Christmas Police!" Sometimes, I mutter it to myself when it's Boxing Day and my cards still haven't gone out, etc. And sometimes I trot out the mantra to comfort friends and family who, under the gun about all things Christmas, could use a little comfort and joy.

I happen to love holiday traditions and rituals, but I try not to be bound by them, generally. However, one that has been non-negotiable through the years is my calling a friend in the nursery business, ordering the biggest, fattest Scotch pine and having it delivered, stand already on, ready for action. I love the convenience and always get exactly what I want. Heck, if I could have it delivered with lights and decorations on it, I would be in holiday heaven.

This year, however, I kept seeing all these tall versions of "Charlie Brown" Christmas trees, as I call them—the trees with sparse branches. While out and about, I began to contemplate a break in tradition (*gasp!*). I went back and forth, weighing pros and cons, wondering if so drastic a departure from the way we've always done it would mean the earth shifting on its axis or other paradigm busters I could contemplate. But I finally resolved to experiment, and dispatched my husband, MacGyver, to find an eight-foot silvertip fir.

When I arrived home that evening, I spotted the radically new form through the window and my heart skipped a beat. This was exciting, this was bracing—a brave new arboreal silhouette! But wait a minute! What was that three-foot silver sphere doing under the tree? Was this some newfangled, quasi-contemporary tree stand? That was NOT happening! On closer inspection, I discovered it was, in fact, a bucket. Turns out, MacGyver, unable to locate an eight-foot silvertip fir, had settled on a five-footer and "grew it" to eight feet with the aid of our galvanized-tin dog food storage bucket.

It took me about a minute to decide how to camouflage the aberration. I grabbed every poinsettia in the house and placed them strategically around the base. *There!* After the lights went up and the cases of decorations were carted up from the basement, I began to place ornaments on the tree.

What usually took a few nights of careful, studied effort was complete in just over an hour. The tree was finished and looked great. I backed away to admire the full effect and fell over one of the many boxes, still full of ornaments—full, since the new shape could only accommodate a fraction of our collection, thereby excluding the use of numerous sentimental, commemorative decorations. This caused not a little conflict in my psyche, not to mention a bruised hip from the fall.

Helping me to my feet, MacG commented that decking the halls was getting to be dangerous. Stifling a stinging retort (it was Christmas, after all), I gently requested that MacG take ALL the leftover boxes back to the basement and promise to remind me of this occasion next year when I next wanted to buck my own tradition. So long, Charlie Brown! No more branching out! ❧

Rose Bush
faces the music in

irish eyes
are laughing

IN THE LAST FEW YEARS, an acronym has surfaced in the zeitgeist: FOMO, which means fear of missing out. It's primarily a young-person thing, I believe, and I pretty much established, on hearing about the phenomena, that I do not suffer from it. This may be due to the fact that my schedule as an editor is rigorous, and if I'm missing something, I'm usually OK with it, except, apparently, when I'm not.

The week of St. Patrick's Day, I flew to Charleston, South Carolina, with an itinerary that would choke a horse—it included social and sales calls, as well as the opportunity to interview a couple of my favorite interior designers individually on the dais of an antiques show. All ready, with almost every minute accounted for, I got a text from another favorite designer, friend, and hostess extraordinaire, asking if I had received her Evite to a St. Patrick's Day brunch, which was taking place the same morning I was due on the dais. I had received it. I had not seen it. I responded that I would be there!

Though it was a tight squeeze, I reasoned thusly: A) She was a good friend and, B) I knew I could do a drive by, see her new digs, hug her neck, imbibe a green drink of some sort (a delicious smoothie, as it turns out), and still make it to the venue seven blocks away in plenty of time. But in this thought process I also realized that, though I was not necessarily AFRAID of missing out, I really didn't want to.

I parked easily around the corner of the home on the main thoroughfare, surprised to find a parking place on such a bustling street. I attended and left the gathering in plenty of time, had it not been St. Patrick's Day.

But on walking out of the party, I heard the sound of brass and percussion instruments playing, "When Irish Eyes are Smiling." Looking down to the end of the street, where the avenue intersected, I spotted a uniformed marching band making their way down the main drag and sidewalks full of enthusiastic citizens and tourists. Which would have been such fun—I mean, I love a parade, except when it prevents me from driving to my next gig.

I quickly looked up my destination and began to hoof it the seven blocks. Now, I don't know if any of you know me, but I'm not young and I was sporting a pair of chic, high-heeled shoes and carrying a heavy tote, so this was no walk in the park. But I made it just in time, skidding in like Kramer on *Seinfeld*, to get miked up and go over my questions. ... Wait, my questions— where were my questions?? Oh yeah, I'd taken my notebook out of my tote before the party, as it was a tad cumbersome. *Yikes!*

But I remembered that, though not of Irish descent, I nonetheless have been blessed with the gift of the gab. And that, combined with good old-fashioned preparation, not to mention charming interviewees, made for a good time. Crisis averted. However, if any future commitments fall on holidays, I'll be sure to check parade routes and maybe get the Uber app. ❧

CPSIA information can be obtained
at www.ICGtesting.com
Printed in the USA
LVOW06*2312140617
538145LV00006B/9/P

9 780984 686421